Funded by the DGLAB/Culture and the Camões, IP – Portugal

REPÚBLICA
PORTUGUESA
CULTURA
DIREÇÃO-GERAL DO LIVRO, DOS ARQUIVOS E
DAS BIBLIOTECAS

CAMÕES
INSTITUTO
DA COOPERAÇÃO
E DA LÍNGUA
PORTUGAL
MINISTÉRIO DOS NEGÓCIOS ESTRANGEIROS

Distributed by Publishers Group West

First Edition

UNDER OUR SKIN

+ A JOURNEY

+ JOAQUIM ARENA

TRANSLATED BY JETHRO SOUTAR

The Unnamed Press
Los Angeles, CA

UNDER OUR SKIN

ONE

And then out of the blue a lady stands up and raises issues of race, bringing to the fore matters that would usually be marginalized. She has dark skin and silver hair and introduces herself as a retired secondary school teacher. Her voice is smooth as porcelain, and she speaks with that mixture of charm and candor you get in older women who are past caring for courtesies. She points out that there were more Black slaves in Portugal than in any other country in Europe.

We're at Belmonte Palace, in Lisbon, on the top of the hill by the castle, where a group of writers and academics have gathered for a conference on the history of the city. Some of the delegates are "French authors of international renown," according to the program, and many have abandoned the cold that still grips their homelands in the European north to bask in the first days of Portuguese spring. Today's discussion focuses on the presence of Black slaves in the city, going back through the centuries and identifying traces of them in the toponymy of today. An image of the painting *Chafariz d'El Rei* (*The King's Fountain*) is projected onto a wall behind the stage. Concepts of Lusophone miscegenation have the historians enthralled.

But the woman with the silver hair, whom I will come to know as Leopoldina, talks about the people in the painting as if they're old acquaintances: Blacks, slaves, Moors; men and women; names and dates. She even speculates on how one ought to pronounce sixteenth-century Portuguese and what the era's most common insults and curses would have been. She wears a brown shawl draped over a knitted white cardigan, denim jeans, and brown cowboy boots, a look that initially strikes me as being almost too neo-hippie. Later on, during one of the breaks, I see her flicking through a book about rice cultivation in the palace library.

A few days earlier, I'd received an unexpected phone call. Besides the experts in the field and the distinguished men and women of letters, the organizers thought they ought to invite someone to represent the ethnic minorities of what remains a predominantly white city. Much to my surprise, that someone was me.

The organizers couldn't have known it, but the representative they'd chosen—a mixed-race man from São Vicente, Cape Verde, an archipelago off the west coast of Africa that was colonized by Portugal—was in the midst of a historical reckoning of his own. I'd recently returned to Portugal, brought back by a death, and was experiencing a profound sense of guilt for having abandoned the country of my birth for a second time. I'd become preoccupied with matters of heritage and background: how my ancestral trajectory was both personal and typical—one more family of Cape Verdean immigrants—and how, in some abstract way, perhaps through that sense of melancholy we Portuguese speakers call *saudade*, my own journey was connected to that first voyage, in 1444, when 235 Africans were brought to Portugal with shackles on their feet.

At the end of the morning session, when speakers and delegates head for lunch, I pick up the printout of *Chafariz d'El Rei* and walk down the hill to Alfama, to see what remains of the fountain depicted in the historic painting.

Unexpected emotion wells up in me as I walk. The people of this picture would've had no idea they were being watched and reproduced on canvas; indeed, it would doubtless have come as a surprise to learn their insignificant existence had even been noticed. What would the painter have been thinking? An anonymous foreign artist who, at some point between 1560 and 1580, decided to compose a street scene in a manner then typical of northern European painting, and inadvertently produced a picture of unparalleled documentary value.

The mediocre quality of the artwork—there is no avoiding the fact that the artist had more enthusiasm than talent—is more than compensated for by its importance as a historical record. Of the 136 people depicted—who, yes, I took the trouble to count— seventy-nine are Black, including seven children caught up in the hustle and bustle of the adults. At first glance, it is unclear if any of these people are captives; indeed, I'd say considerable effort is made by some of them to hide this fateful fact, or at least to ignore it. They're taking part in the daily routine of queuing to fill up water jars, as many as could feasibly be carried, while indulging in a little conversation. It doesn't take too much imagination to hear the cacophony of voices exclaiming in Balanta, Papel, Manjak, Mandinka, Fulani, Beafada, Serer, Soninke, and Mende, joking and laughing, protesting and consoling, lamenting lives that had nothing to offer them, Black men and women—and slaves, besides.

I can almost smell the odors coming from their bodies, awkwardly wrapped in European clothes. The water girls look sensual in their bright, long skirts, the pitchers on their heads likely one of the details that most caught the painter's attention. The artist would probably never have seen so many Black people gathered together—noisily, festively, lewdly—in a public space before. Sixteenth-century Lisbon was like nowhere else in Europe, populous but with wide-open spaces, a city that had nourished and reinvented itself thanks to the arrival of spices from new worlds. Little wonder the outsider felt compelled to arrange a street scene containing such unusual sights.

The Chafariz d'El Rei itself occupies the right-hand side of the painting, the artist being primarily concerned with the world that revolved around the fountain's six spouts, each one painted white and shaped like a horse's head. Above them, three arched vaults are supported by two pillars, likewise painted white, creating an atrium sixty feet long and thirty feet deep. The pillars and the vaults, as well as the terrace above the arches—where plants can be seen growing, lilies perhaps—are adorned in Moorish style with carvings and decorative flourishes. The middle arch features the royal coat of arms at its center, and the two side arches bear the heads of animals of some kind. The fountain's entire portico, broad enough to shelter anyone who might have to spend several hours queuing there, is tucked in between two towers left over from the ancient Cerca Moura city wall.

The good reputation enjoyed by the water in the area was likewise ancient. The Roman architect and engineer Vitruvius references Lisbon's eastern waters in book eight of his *De architectura*, a volume dedicated to hydraulic constructions. ʿAbd al-Muʾmin, the first caliph of the Almohad empire, wrote a description of Lisbon in the twelfth century in which he highlighted the city's famous hot springs (*al-hamma*, in the Arabic, which gave the Alfama neighborhood its name). Three centuries later, the Portuguese humanist philosopher Damião de Góis was equally impressed by the fountain, praising the construction of its columns and arches and the quality of its water, "pure and fresh and a great pleasure to drink."

As the painting shows, the fountain previously opened out into a rectangular space, a sort of town square built on slightly lower ground to the road. Some people linger and chat in a leisurely manner at the foot of two stone steps, while others seem to loiter with no intent other than to quench their thirst and catch the latest gossip. A man makes expressive gestures, as if calling out to someone. At center stage, a Black man and a white woman seem ahead of their time in dancing a sort of tango together. Two men, New Christians perhaps, appear to be weighing up the risks of an ambitious commercial venture, as befitted Lisbon's glorious days of old. On the right, three bearded men look on as a majestic knight rides past. And as if to prove that, irrespective of time or latitude, there's always more to things than meets the eye, this horseman is Black.

The men's apparent curiosity and gnostic acceptance of the enigmatic figure, dressed in a cloak of the Order of Santiago, echoes the painter's evident fascination. The loftiness of the knight's position and the elegance of his horse—a sacred animal—give him a dignity above and beyond all the other people in the painting, thus undermining the entire social order the scene prescribes.

Who can he be, this chevalier, violating established norms with his nobility? Can what these half dozen brushstrokes suggest actually be true? Could a Black man really have become a knight of the Order of Santiago?

The order was a military/religious group founded in Spain in the twelfth century to protect pilgrims on the way to Santiago de Compostela and the shrine of Saint James (*Tiago* in Spanish and Portuguese equates to "James"), a route now popularly known as the Camino. A Portuguese chapter, known as the Order of Saint James of the Sword, was soon established, with membership restricted to noblemen. There would eventually be three such orders in Portugal—Saint James of the Sword, Avis, and Christ—and all had similarly exclusive rules of entry, but they occasionally made exceptions. Francis A. Dutra, an American scholar of early modern Portugal, has studied these orders, and his findings provide clues as to who this Black knight might be.

In the early eighteenth century, a record was compiled of all the men who'd required special dispensation to gain knighthoods in the three orders. These dispensations were divided into different categories—age, illegitimacy, ancestry, and so on—with twenty-seven names listed under "*Mulato* and / or Descended from African slaves." Most were biracial, the descendants of the sort of people shown in the *Chafariz* painting, but Dutra determined that seven of them were Black: one in the Order of Avis, three in the Order of Christ, and three in the Order of Saint James. Dutra also notes that Manuel Gonçalves Doria, a soldier born in Brazil, was the first Afro-Brazilian to become a knight of the Order of Saint James, but that was not until 1628, many years after the painting.

Of the three Black men awarded knighthoods of Saint James of the Sword, two were noblemen from royal households, while the third, João de Sá Panasco, was a court jester descended from slaves. Given this background, Panasco is, it is argued, the most likely of the three to have frequented the fountain area. The man in the painting also fits what we know of Panasco's description: the clothes, the stance, the touch of gray in the hair.

If it is Panasco—and it's widely held that it is—then his parading through the square, a meeting place for Black men and women at the heart of the kingdom, acquires a certain poetic quality. Born in the Congo, Panasco was brought to Lisbon as a boy and put to work in several houses before finding his way into the court of King João III and Catherine of Austria. There he became a habitual presence at the royal table, appreciated for his amusing jokes and stories, and known for his witty and spirited retorts if mocked: "For the Portuguese gent, happiness consists of being called Vasconçelos, owning an estate, having six hundred thousand réis of monthly income, and being stupid and useless."

Panasco was certainly much more than a "fly in the milk," as Dom Francisco Coutinho, the Count of Redondo, described him after finding him sick in bed, wrapped in white sheets. In 1535, while still a teenager, he was sent to North Africa, under the command of the king's brother, Prince Luís, as part of the Portuguese contingent in Charles V's Conquest of Tunis. In the siege that followed the sinking of the sea fleet of Hayreddin Barbarossa, Panasco noticed a small dog sitting frightened under an olive tree. Impervious to the cavalry charges and flying arrows, Panasco rode across the battlefield and picked up the puppy, an Anatolian shepherd that he took back to Lisbon and looked after for the rest of his days.

Panasco was awarded the habit of the Order of Saint James for his services to the crown sometime between 1550 and 1557. In later life, however, ground down by racist attitudes and the stigma of his background, he became overwhelmed with bitterness and took to drink. Looking at the painting again, I wonder what the other Black people, the slaves and free slaves he crossed paths with in the royal court or on the city streets, made of him. He was a man without a mask, but at the time this made for a split personality.

The painting also depicts a number of Portuguese worthies, including noblemen, some of them standing, others on horseback and dressed in black. Two policemen carry away a drunken Black man, a detail mentioned by Leopoldina at the conference: alcohol-related depravity prompted the Lisbon Town Hall to ban Black people from drinking wine in taverns or indeed from entering them. Alcoholism was actually a double vice, for slaves were forbidden from carrying money or having possessions of any kind, meaning that if they were to buy wine, they would have to steal.

Black slaves were not considered people but things: in Portuguese there is a distinction between the word *negro*, which describes a Black person, and *preto*, which describes a black thing; Black slaves were called *pretos*. (For this reason, *negro* is not taken to be an offensive term in Portuguese, whereas *preto* continues to be used as a racist slur.) "Things" could not buy other things, like wine. Nor could they ride around on horses, not least because being mounted conveyed indisputable dignity, in this case the dignity of a knight.

Elsewhere in the picture, a young Black man is rowing a boat while another shakes a tambourine, doubtless making the pleasure cruise being enjoyed by a white couple that bit more pleasurable. Another Black man stands with a pot over his head, perhaps performing some kind of street theater.

Protagonism aside, it's worth clarifying that, with the exception of Panasco, all the Black men and women in the picture are preserved for posterity like nonspecific blackbirds. Their heads are mostly jet-black blurs with barely defined eyes, ears, noses, or mouths, as if the artist could only reflect the church decree that Black people had no souls.

If the Christian hereafter was a place of gardens and angels, then the pagan one was a sea of shadows and chill winds. Having no soul denied Black people salvation and excluded them from the grounds of Christian cemeteries. Their destiny was the Poço dos Negros (literally the "Blacks' Well," though it was a mere pit) and the "lime shroud," a colloquialism born of the fact that the pit was periodically disinfected with quicklime.

As I walk the city streets now, it's hard to imagine the stench of dead bodies that would have floated in the air then, entering homes and getting up the noses of noblemen and commoners alike. Lisbon would have been a filthy place, polluted as much by credo and small-mindedness as by lack of hygiene. After being dumped in the pit, bodies were smothered in salt, lest their rotting flesh and exposed bones contaminate the city's water and spoil the pure, fresh taste that Damião de Góis had described.

The 1444 shipment of enslaved Africans landed at Lagos, in the Algarve, but some of the 235 men, women, and children were brought to Lisbon. They were the spoils of raids in Arguin and Guinea, transported by men in the employ of Prince Henry the Navigator. The prince's men had to overcome adversity—fighting, killing, and fettering—to deliver their cargo, and, as they saw it, they managed to do so because the Good Lord favored them over all other living creatures, not least the seminaked savages who'd vainly sought to hide their children in dusty fields. Those 235 were the first of their kind to experience the strange place of exile that was the Europe of Christ and salvation.

Back then, before the Poço dos Negros was established on the king's orders in 1515, Black cadavers were tossed without ceremony, never mind rites, into the Santa Catarina ravine. There they were feasted on by stray dogs and pulverized by the waves of the Rio Tejo that lapped the shore on stormy nights.

I try to imagine what the older Black people, those who recalled the idyll of their African kingdoms, must have thought of fifteenth-century Lisbon. I imagine their faces overwhelmed with sorrow, their bodies and hearts gripped with cold, but not the least stirring of revolt. Their sense of alienation and instinct for survival must have been tremendous, but any notion of returning to the rivers of their youth would have been beaten out of them by the first winter they spent on the city's streets. They reconciled themselves to lives as human beasts of burden, performing mechanical work and adoring the new god of heaven and hell, of colorful parades and shiny possessions.

Leaving the fountain, I head down Rua da Alfândega (Customs-house Street), retracing routes as old as the city's first street maps. People queue outside restaurants waiting for a table and the prospect of grilled sardines, a popular dish in the area since at least the sixteenth century. There used to be a market space here with food shacks known as Malcozinhado (literally "badly cooked"), where people of all races gathered and ate, the workingmen and -women who kept the city ticking over: the 250 coal men, Black and white, who unloaded the coal ships and delivered sacks about town; the 150 Black dockers; the 200 Black boys who hawked fish and meat from baskets; the 1,000 Black female water vendors; the 40 Black and Moorish trappers; the 50 Black whitewashers; and, last but not least, the 1,000 Black "gong farmers" who collected the city's waste and tipped it into the river every morning. At the conference, Leopoldina had just referenced these people, logged in records kept by João Brandão, one of King João III's valets, in the late sixteenth century.

Back near the fountain I hear Asian languages spoken at the doors of shops run by Pakistani men, and I cannot help but marvel at the strange routes humans have traveled since the beginning of time. Tourist couples wander up and down the road, taking photos and lingering in front of the fountain, trying to decipher a plaque carved into the stone of the wall:

CHAFARIZ D'EL REI

BUILT IN THE 13TH CENTURY,

RENOVATED BY KING DOM DINIS,

REBUILT IN 1747,

REPAIRED AFTER THE 1755 EARTHQUAKE,

AND UPGRADED IN THE MID-19TH CENTURY.

The spouts in the form of horses' heads disappeared long ago, and no one comes here to collect water anymore. The fountain is classified as a national heritage building and a place of public interest, "along with its corresponding hydraulic structures (tank, cistern, and water shaft), situated on Rua do Cais de Santarém, at the junction between Chafariz d'El Rei and São João da Praça, in the parish of Sé, Lisbon, in the town and municipality of Lisbon, duly designated a special protection zone."

These days the fountain looks more like a marble mausoleum, weathered and withered with time. The current facade, a piece of bleak classicist architecture dating from 1864, juts out from beneath the Palacete Chafariz d'El Rei (King's Fountain Palace), a work of neo-Moorish splendor that now serves as an upscale "Home Boutique Hotel." On the veranda, where on that gray day in the sixteenth century two ladies hung bedspreads out to air, a magnificent bougainvillea tumbles down toward the fountain roof. I look again at the lilies in the picture and wonder whether this floral detail is the most consistent element connecting the painting with the modern reality of the place.

As I raise my hands to take a photo of the bougainvillea, a middle-aged man suddenly appears on the hotel veranda. "I'm the king of the waters," he shouts down to me in English.

I

Six months earlier death comes knocking at my door from two thousand miles away. I'm sitting at my desk when I get the news. I try to get the images I have in my head to focus: the man who tried to be my father for over thirty years; the son I've pretended to be my whole life. My father, officially, not biologically, and not anymore. A death that will nevertheless force me back to Lisbon to help settle his affairs, just when I thought I'd made these dry and sleepy islands my home.

The news from Portugal speaks of cold mornings and even of snow in Lisbon, rare indeed. My adoptive father was found in a building that was undergoing renovation work. The owner let homeless people spend the night there when it got particularly cold. My father was lying on his side, uncovered, hunched up, fully clothed and wearing shoes. He had plastic bags beside him containing a few odds and ends, and an old suitcase. He wore denim trousers, and his belt and fly were undone. It had looked as if he were asleep, laid out on a mattress, his back against the wall.

People who live in sunny climates are said to be dreamier than those who live in the cold, but maybe there's just more time for reveries. The general slowness makes energetic thinkers of us all. It's also claimed that days are more suited to reflection in the tropics. For the many Cape Verdeans who lead their lives elsewhere, governed by the European clock, reflection is an almost alien concept. But unlike in, say, England or the Netherlands, here on São Vicente, we can experience luxury in the form of a simple shadow. We are, therefore, less materialistic than others, but that's not only because of the sleepy dryness of the islands. There's a sort of metaphysical restlessness that stimulates creativity here too, especially when it comes to music. Despite the isolation, the vastness of the big blue sky and the ocean gives us a sense of continuity, an appreciation of the light that bathes all human beings and a conviction that we too will get to dip our spoons into the Christian soup cauldron.

So what does being tropical mean? Being less concrete and assertive in our ideas and convictions? There's certainly an art to filling the arid hours and empty nights here.

The bad news reaches me first thing in the morning. I retreat to the intimacy of my bookshelves, while outside the day quickly passes from fresh to mild to the start of a heat wave. It's absurd to try to fit the news of someone's death into the context of whatever story you have in hand, some false pseudo-writerly sense of abstract anguish. But as I flick through my books, it's as if a ghost has settled between the lines and started hopping from noun to pronoun, though doubtless verbs could take it further. How many lives are supported by these spines? How many possibilities of what it is to be human are contained within the gray matter of these pages?

My library is my cathedral, and today it serves as my confessional. There's something extraordinary about the way writers can continue to speak to us from beyond the grave. Men and women who write set out to explore someone else's perspective and see the world through other people's eyes. They place literature at the center of their lives. The least I can do is afford them a few minutes of concentration every day. Perhaps

I believe they offer the prospect of a different landscape, like the merchant who carries an unknown magic spice in his pouch or the traveler who crosses deserts armed with the secret weapon of literacy. Words, carefully chosen, speak louder than actions; they are actions. They emerge from the writer's pen to become the sublime and revolutionary act of literature: they disrupt reality and refashion it, for deep down everyone knows how riddled by mistakes and paradoxes reality is.

I think about the artifice involved in describing the world and the human condition in endless combinations of twenty-six letters, and the way even the same combinations can convey anger and hate or love and kindness, depending on the intentions of whoever's wielding them. How these combinations help us define things, contemplate mysteries, and pass on memories, such as those of the journeys my stepfather went on throughout his life, registered in letters posted to us from faraway countries, his handwriting hard to decipher, his Portuguese faltering but full of the best intentions; waves of black ink as choppy as the seas he sailed.

Everything suddenly becomes clearer to me.

The page I have open before me melts away, and I see myself walking through a garden with him, alongside other fathers leading other children by the hand, and I don't have the courage to tell him that the shoes he bought for me are too tight and hurt my toes. Maybe I'm too touched by his generosity to speak up. And now, on the day of his death, caught in the undertow of the moment itself, I feel moved again, for none of this was inevitable. I put the book back on the shelf and sit down in my rocking chair, trying to digest the end of a life as calmly as possible, the end of a man.

The wind lifts the curtains and blows dust across the floor, a fine dust that coats every house on the island. No sooner have you swept it up than more moves in, gathers in every crook and cranny, every corner of your memory. It's a losing battle right from the start.

Faced with the mundane facts, I imagine an "ideal" end for him: perhaps a bloody crime that might afford him some glory at the last, like some dazzling detail on a dead flower.

But all I really feel is anger at his impudence.

I leave the house and go for a walk, willing time and space to force out the grief I want to have in me. I pass a group of students singing, watch a flock of birds score through the cloudless sky. It's winter in Lisbon, but here in Cape Verde the sun beats down on everything with heavy and somber rays. For a brief moment I recall our life in Portugal all those years ago, picturing it all neat and tidy: a tranquil home with items in their proper places; compartments for everything, including our shadows. The mothball smell of his suitcase suddenly comes to me, his personal affairs, his perfumes and aftershaves, until I turn around, change course, and head up the road toward Bairro da Ribeira Bote and the house where he was born.

Through a chink in the door, I see a young teacher on a wooden bench, a dozen children sitting on the cement floor before him, a magnificent poem written on the chalkboard. I'm struck by the spirit of schoolmasters the world over, preparing their charges for life. The building is in a fairly bad state. The people who use or live in it now have plastered cement and whitewash here and there, while the neighborhood youth have fashioned a gym with barbells in the yard. A young prostitute lives in the annex room at the back, her eyes moist, a red rose tattooed on her chest.

When you think about it, almost all cultures see adoption as a noble act. That doesn't mean it's not still a strange decision, volunteering to correct an anomaly in a family's makeup, filling a void in a child's life but often without bothering to ask what the child thinks about it first. Overflowing with elastic love to the point that you forsake your own freedom to assume the responsibilities of a parent, without the slightest idea of whether you're suited to the task. Which of course is all very different from, say, the Roman consul in *Ben Hur* adopting Judah as his son, after the galley slave (a tan and chiseled Charlton Heston) saves his life in a shipwreck.

For the child involved, adoption, or a parent remarrying, inevitably engenders a brutal paradox. This is especially true when the child knows of the existence of an absent biological parent, in this case the father, and in my case a father who existed only in my imagination, for he left us when I was two, returning to Portugal, unable to juggle the demands of having two families anymore. But the stepchild will always likely harbor the fantasy of the "real" father returning one day. What happens then? Will the two fathers clash, fight to the death for custody of the child?

Incorporating new family members in the form of half brothers and sisters is commonplace in Cape Verde, as it is elsewhere in times of hunger, war, or poverty. But despite being common, and even when the new family home presents itself as an oasis, there is still a tension, for there is always drama involved, a backstory of hardship, misfortune, or abuse.

Clarinha became my mother's half sister during the terrible famines that plagued Cape Verde in the 1940s. Perhaps as a result, when my mother speaks of Clarinha now, she expresses much more love than when she speaks of her biological sister, my aunt Manuela.

When I was around eight or nine, I got an early glimpse of what love looks like for an adopted child. It was in a bar in central Lisbon, on a trip into town that seesawed between the wishes of adult and child. My new stepfather introduced me to his friends, spread out across various tables and the bar, some of them playing cards. I remember someone laughing and saying your boy looks white. A fog seemed to descend, and I tried to make it go away. I tugged at my stepfather's arm, wanting to rescue us from the unsettling situation. But he seemed to embrace the discomfort, and his friends ruffled my hair and tweaked my ears, and I stoically went along with this uninvited display of paternal pride.

One day not long after that, I opened his wardrobe and found coats designed to withstand cold winters in northern Europe or America. I pictured myself dressed in those animal hides, crossing frozen rivers and lakes on board an icebreaker. Alongside the coats was a woolen fisherman's sweater with a turtleneck, like the one Ernest Hemingway wears in the famous photo by Yousuf Karsh. The wardrobe smelled strongly of adventure.

And in this way, I shyly began to approach my substitute father, a man who spent most of his life on tankers (not to mention tanked up) and came in and out of my life as regularly as the changing of the seasons. He was a sailor, that staple of *Boy's Own* legends, and I duly projected a comic-book heroism onto him, a heroism that would have been impossible for anyone to live up to.

That night I gaze out over the bay of Porto Grande and the lights of boats reflected in the water, twinkling in the silence, like flags without masts fallen from Monte Cara. It was here that the landscape of my childhood changed forever.

There's no question that time is our biggest killer, and that if a man lets an abyss open up inside him, only he himself can cross it. My stepfather has breathed his last breath, and I'm left wondering whether the stones on the pavement outside remember the weight of his body, the weight of defeat that had accompanied him for quite some time. The hardest part isn't imagining him dead, lying cold and heavy, sleeping rough on a mattress. I find it much more painful to imagine him as a child—the restless and mischievous child I'm told he was—a habit I've had since my own childhood that surfaces whenever an adult close to me dies. For now, I fix on the image of how my stepfather's face and body used to shake when he laughed, as he struggled to regain his composure. The last gasp, a final self-portrait on a cold morning cut short. Ultimately we can never tell if the images that pass across our retinas are external or if we've conjured them up ourselves.

A few days later, I begin my return.

I abandon the island of my birth, where I've spent the last few years trying to recover the life denied to me as the child of emigrants, trying to solve the age-old problem of my identifying skin. Lisbon and Portugal ended up being forgotten about for a while. I made new friends, met people who brought added color and feeling into my life. I traveled around the different islands, walked up winding mountain paths, contemplated the sleepy ruins of long-abandoned houses, family homes now haunted by the memories of children like me, people who upped sticks one day and never came back. Maybe I'd been waiting for a good reason to bring this stage of my life to an end, some unavoidable obligation to move on, because although I didn't want to give it up, I knew it couldn't last forever, nothing ever does. My stepfather's death felt like the logical conclusion. Sometimes that's all we're waiting for: a strong wind to blow in from the north, pick us up, and transport us to another hemisphere.

I'd come back to Cape Verde to fulfill a wish, but it was an idealized life and now it's run its course. Now it's time to reclaim my other life, the one waiting for me back in Lisbon, the one where I follow in the footsteps of the man pretending to be me.

TWO

And such is the random chaos of life that a few weeks later I bump into the silver-haired lady from the conference on the train. I'm on my way back to Lisbon from an exhibition in Cascais entitled *Os negros no coração do império (Blacks at the Heart of the Empire)*. She's clutching a brochure like mine, and as we get talking, we realize we must have just missed each other. We talk about the exhibition: the reproductions and the information panels, the range of historical testimonies and fragments of a muffled history, and the sense we'd both had of traveling back in time as we moved through the different rooms. Walking through the exhibition, we'd felt like invisible extras, staring into the absent eyes of people performing insignificant tasks, their souls stripped of dignity. But the more one wandered between victims and perpetrators, slaves and slavers, the more unreal it seemed, as if this had all happened in a different country on another continent.

Nevertheless, by the end of it, we'd both emerged feeling slightly relieved that despite the suffocating injustice of it all, contact between the cultures had proved hugely enriching; that in spite of the humiliations and cruelties, the outline of a renewed culture had emerged through imperceptible interpenetration and the clash between different peoples. This, we agreed, was precisely why the period, so decisive in our history, should not be deemed too awkward to deal with and conveniently filed away:

these things did and do exist and cannot be erased; they must be faced up to.

Compelled by a universalist spirit that only grew after her retirement from teaching, Leopoldina has since dedicated herself to researching the presence of Africans in Portugal and the social structures they inhabited. She tells me that, as a hobby, her fascination with history's shadows can prove greatly rewarding: she's regularly amazed by the things she finds that had been kept hidden. But it is nevertheless a hobby: "I'm strictly an amateur, I'm not planning on publishing an academic thesis or anything."

I'd been immediately impressed by her erudition at the conference, but now I suspect there's something else too: her passion for Black history in Portugal seems special somehow, personal. When I ask her, she answers somewhat enigmatically: "It runs in the blood."

As the train speeds on, she insists she's just an old spinster who lives alone in a basement flat on one of Lisbon's many hills, the oldest and only survivor of three sisters. A niece usually visits her on the weekends, but she spends most days in the library. When the weather's nice she likes to walk around Belém.

Upon her suggestion, we meet for lunch in Belém a few days later. As we walk past the Jerónimos Monastery, Leopoldina asks me about my family and our immigrant story. We discuss the Cape Verdean families who arrived by the dozen in the 1960s, moving into derelict flats in Lisbon's city center, and how their neighbors, some of whom had witnessed the birth of the Portuguese Republic in 1910, sneered at the new arrivals, no doubt suspecting they were related to the rebels then fighting Portuguese soldiers in the Colonial Wars, or the Wars of Independence, as they were known in the colonized countries themselves.

Leopoldina leads us toward the Tropical Botanical Garden, formerly the Colonial Garden, not far from the monastery. We pass through the iron gates and wander up a path lined with listless palm trees and alive with birdsong.

"This is one of the few places in the city where I feel happy and at peace," she tells me.

Clouds of insects and dragonflies hover over a lake where white-feathered ducks with red beaks swim through the green water. After the palm trees come the horsetail trees, brought from Brazil and Argentina, followed by clumps of bamboo and Judas trees, which Leopoldina introduces me to as if they are old friends. The sculpted heads of two Black boys sit atop pillars, relics from the 1940 Portuguese World Exhibition, at the approach to an old one-story house with a red-tiled roof.

"It's a shame they let the greenhouse go to ruin," Leopoldina observes.

Much of the garden lives in the permanent shade of inter-connecting trees; it's like being in a rain forest.

"*Melaleuca lanceolata* (*Myrtaceae*)," says Leopoldina, pointing to a plaque beneath a tree. "Isn't it a pretty name?"

We sit on a stone bench nearby. The intimacy of the moment brings back teenage memories of sharing benches with girls for the first time. Directly in front of us is the largest tree trunk I've ever seen. The shadow created by the tree's crown must be at least two hundred feet in diameter, though the tree itself is less than a hundred feet tall. Its giant, snaking roots slide over the ground for sixty feet before burying themselves into the earth. Every few seconds a piece of dried fruit falls from the tree and lands on the carpet of dead leaves with a thud.

"It's my favorite tree," Leopoldina says, "*Ficus religiosa*, from the Asian tropics, better known as the sacred fig or peepal tree."

We remain silent for a while, an odd couple listening to the beat of the falling fruit. Then Leopoldina tells me the real reason she went to the conference at Belmonte Palace.

"My great-great-great-grandmother, a woman named Catarina, was a slave in the first Count of Belmonte's house," she says. "The man's name was Dom Vasco Manuel de Figueiredo Cabral da Câmara, until Queen Dona Maria I made him a count in 1767. As a child I was told stories of how he mistreated Catarina to such an extent that the law had to intervene, and how his wife threatened to sell her to Maranhão, in Brazil, which must have hastened her decision to run away. The story of her escape was always being told over dinner and was thus passed down through the generations. I've looked into it, and she seems to have been born in Dom Fradique's Court, the house the count lived in before Belmonte Palace was built, just before the Freedom of Wombs Law."

The Freedom of Wombs Law was introduced by the Marquis of Pombal in 1773. It decreed that, henceforth, any child born to an enslaved mother in Portugal would be born free. Prior to that, despite a 1761 law forbidding the import of slaves to Portugal, if you were born to an enslaved mother already there, you were born enslaved. The law also made a tentative attempt to redress this by declaring that any slave then living in Portugal, having been born into slavery and whose parents, grandparents, and great-grandparents had likewise been slaves, could claim his or her freedom.

This law, added to the 1761 law, marked the beginning of the end of slavery in Portugal, but no more than the beginning. Slavery was definitively outlawed throughout the Portuguese empire, Portugal included, only in 1869. In other words, if Catarina had been born in, say, 1772, the year before the Freedom of Wombs Law, she would have had to live to the ripe old age of ninety-seven before she tasted liberty.

"In any case," Leopoldina continues, "we know she was part of a group of Black slaves that fled Lisbon one morning in the early nineteenth century, heading south and crossing the marshes of the Rio Sado valley, then settling on a hillside near the modern-day village of São Romão, where I was born a hundred years later."

They arrived in São Romão, Catarina and her companions, bedraggled and with scant belongings. On the Herdade dos Frades estate, they were put to work in the fields alongside Blacks and whites already established there. Poor white families had come from elsewhere in Portugal to clear scrubland and work the remote Alentejo fields generations ago. The Black families were a more recent presence. When rice cultivation was introduced to the area in the late eighteenth century, malaria became rife. Leaning into the claim that Africans were more resistant to the fevers than Europeans, the rice growers sought out Black slaves to work the diseased swamps where whites refused to go.

Josefa, Leopoldina's great-great-grandmother, was born in São Romão in 1820. What's known of her comes care of Leopoldina's grandmother Eugénia, who had a prodigious memory and knew Josefa as a child. Josefa was an old woman by then, the latter years of the nineteenth century, and Eugénia was just a little girl, but Eugénia garnered further details from her mother, Zulmira, Leopoldina's great-grandmother. Eugénia passed these details on to Leopoldina through stories: how Josefa helped with weeding the rice fields even as a very young girl; how she liked to wear a straw hat and tucked wildflowers into its black band; how she helped build the seedbeds for the rice, after the family had labored for months to clear the land. When Josefa wasn't working, she would make scarecrows to frighten the birds away and stop them from eating the seed.

All the Black people on the hill were poor, like most farmhands in the region. At the end of the weeding season, the boss would give them a lamb and everyone would chip in to buy wine, and there would be a communal meal, usually a big broth. Their hard toil was forgotten for a day, and they ate and drank and sang the boss's praises. The Black workers improvised drums out of bowls and called up ancestral chants. At the beginning of summer and after the harvest, Josefa's family would travel by horse and cart to see the saint's day festivals in the nearby town of Alcácer do Sal.

Josefa was a typical country girl, by turns rugged, rebellious, and sweet, a defenseless look forever on her face. When she was fifteen, she fell in love with a man named Domingos, who'd been a soldier in the Absolutist infantry in the Portuguese Civil War. The war had ended two years earlier, with the Absolutists losing out to the Liberals, but he still went around with a pistol and a dagger under his coat. Josefa liked his tough-guy image and was charmed by his sense of humor. They would meet at dusk by the well farthest from the village or under the cork trees on the other side of the hill. One day he told her he was going to join the armed uprising about to start in the Algarve mountains. He promised to come back and visit her whenever he could, asking her to trust in his return and saying he had a debt to honor with his former commander. Without further ado, he rode off into the autumn evening light.

Weeks passed, then months, without any word from Domingos. Josefa worked the fields to bury her anguish and sought comfort in the beauty of the estate's meadows. But time dragged on, the summer winds came, and still she'd had no news of him.

One day in Alcácer do Sal, Josefa heard people say that several cities in the Algarve had been attacked and plundered by Absolutist guerrilla fighters. A few nights later she sensed a presence outside her bedroom window, and when she went out to look, Domingos emerged from behind the bushes. They embraced as she frantically sought out signs of injury, but he was healthy and full of smiles. Things were going well, he said, the commander was smart and Domingos was a good shot. They lay on the earth together until dawn, when he dried her tears, got back on his horse, and vanished into the half-light.

She saw that a future with Domingos was still possible and that her life lay ahead of her, not behind her. She started to find any excuse she could to go into Alcácer do Sal and hear the latest news, accounts of sieges and battles. She heard that a group of Absolutist rebels had crossed into the Alentejo and attacked the villages of Cercal and Vila Nova de Milfontes.

Domingos had promised that overthrowing the Liberals would make him a wealthy man, a landowner in the Lower Alentejo. But the Liberal government refused to be cowed by the guerrilla attacks. The Algarve's mountain inhabitants were ordered to take refuge in the cities and to take their work tools with them, as a Liberal cavalry regiment docked in Lagos, well armed and raring to go. A few days later, Remexido, the Absolutist rebel leader, was captured and shot with a group of loyalists. Josefa cried out when she heard the news, but calmed when she learned there wasn't a Black man among them. Nevertheless, the trauma took its toll: the stress of waiting showed in her tired face and eyes, and she acquired the hardened look of those who know everything can be lost from one moment to the next.

But after further skirmishes with the army, the last rebel soldiers surrendered in exchange for a royal pardon. Domingos rode through the night in order to collapse into Josefa's arms. They married soon after that, and Domingos became a farmhand in the marshlands.

"My great-great-grandfather was a very lucky man," Leopoldina concludes.

We meet up again another day, and after walking her home, Leopoldina invites me into her flat. A photo of her mother, taken on a visit to the Caldas da Rainha bathhouses in 1938, takes pride of place on a cabinet. The woman's dark face and curly hair unmistakably indicate her origins. The walls of the flat are adorned with prints of famous paintings—*The Crying Boy, The Virgin Mary, Christ and the Sacred Heart*—and old plates. An ancient television set, which Leopoldina says she rarely uses, sits on a black wooden chest. Wild horses cross a river in an oil painting hung above holy pictures, and a dresser displaying glass knicknacks and giant bronze flies. A dado rail of blue-and-white tiles with images of a wine harvest divides the walls in half.

The window gives a view of the shins and knees of people passing by on the sidewalk outside. Leopoldina says it's amazing how you learn to recognize people by the firmness of their footsteps, their dainty elegance, or their dragging heels. She hibernates in October, pulling the blinds down permanently until spring. At the height of summer, if she forgets to close the window, the wind blows in all sorts of things: newspapers, leaflets, leaves, cigarette ends. But winter or summer, day or night, she always has to have the lights switched on, and the place is constantly damp.

Leopoldina opens a desk drawer and takes out an A5 sheet on which she's drawn a family tree, or rather three trees whose branches are fused and intertwined. She shows me a long list of names of children, grandchildren, great-grandchildren, and great-great-grandchildren, along with dates of births, deaths, marriages, all connected to branches that often start or finish with a question mark. The margins are full of notes and additional details, sending forth an army of numbers and asterisks attached to particular names and dates. She runs me through the various marriages, but I become quickly overwhelmed with information and utterly lost. I watch on, all the same, admiring her enthusiasm. She homes in on Catarina to show me how the law and society changed over the generations, bringing her great-great-great-grandmother if not justice, then the first degree of equity.

That evening, as I'm leaving, I help Leopoldina put out the building's communal garbage can. It's a daily task, she explains, that befalls her as the resident of the basement flat, "as if I'm some kind of sweet old concierge." A few days later I return, having offered to help clear the overgrown backyard. I spend the afternoon hacking away at the dried-out bushes that rise from her flower beds, then picking lemons and loquats from two semiwild fruit trees, before cutting them back to allow a little extra light and air into the flat. Leopoldina helps by holding the stepladder and telling me funny stories.

She's light on her feet for someone of seventy-eight and has a sharp sense of humor. But she's not above asking for help. I continue to return to her flat, running occasional errands for her, popping out to the shops to fetch onions, garlic, strawberries, savory pies. When I get back, she reads me passages from her notes and research. She leads a solitary life, but she still gets a great kick out of watching detective series on TV, and she likes it when a neighbor plays fado records with the windows open. Then there are the caged birds kept on balconies that sing on sunny mornings, and the cats that line up to drink from the trough in her yard.

On another visit, after making me a cup of tea, she opens a book and takes out a picture she keeps tucked inside. She hands it to me mysteriously, saying she found it in a secondhand bookstore on Rua do Alecrim. Two young women pose on a park bench in London, with Saint Paul's Cathedral in the background. One of the women has luminous white skin; her hair is tied up and her left hand holds an open book. Her right hand is placed, with affectionate familiarity, on the leg of the other woman, who is Black.

Both women are pretty, slim, and elegant. Their body language and facial expressions suggest a depiction of friendship, and, this being a painting from the late eighteenth century, the obvious conclusion is that it is a portrait of a young heiress and her favorite maid. Indeed, that was the interpretation until relatively recently, Leopoldina tells me. Then someone noticed that both women are wearing pearls and silk.

The painting was commissioned by William Murray, the first Earl of Mansfield and the lord chief justice, the most powerful judge in England. The two women portrayed are Lady Elizabeth Murray and Dido Elizabeth Belle, and both were Murray's nieces.

Dido's story will be familiar to anyone who's seen *Belle*, the 2013 film directed by Amma Asante and inspired by this painting. Leopoldina, unable to contain her excitement, tells it to me over tea and cake. Dido was born in the Caribbean, the daughter of Maria Belle, an enslaved Black African woman, and Sir John Lindsay, an admiral in the Royal Navy. At the age of five, Dido was sent by Sir John to live with his uncle, Lord Mansfield. The Mansfields, who had no children of their own, were already raising their niece, Lady Elizabeth, whose mother had died. Elizabeth was a year older than Dido, and they were raised and educated as companions at Kenwood House in London.

Leopoldina is amazed that a man of such high public profile and social standing as Lord Mansfield would welcome a young, illegitimate girl of Black origin into his family at that time. Though treated more as a poor relation than an absolute equal, Dido certainly wasn't hidden. Thomas Hutchinson, a former governor of Massachusetts, visited Kenwood House in 1779 and noted in his diary that "a black came in after dinner and sat with the ladies, and after coffee, walked with the company in the gardens, one of the young ladies having her arm within the other."

But it is the possible influence Dido had on Lord Mansfield's attitude toward slavery that makes Leopoldina's gray eyes really light up. The transatlantic slave trade was at its height, and Britain's wealth relied on slave labor in the Caribbean and North America. Nevertheless, Lord Mansfield presided over a number of court cases that challenged the trade's legality, including that of James Somerset, an enslaved man who had attempted to escape when his ship docked in England in 1769. Once captured, he was imprisoned on another ship set to sail to Jamaica, where he would be sold. But Lord Mansfield ordered his case be heard and eventually ruled that it was illegal to transport a slave out of England against his will. Lord Mansfield was careful to focus on the letter of the law rather than on humanitarian principles, but it was speculated, a theory Leopoldina wholeheartedly endorsed, that Dido swayed his judgment.

Lord Mansfield later heard the case of the so-called *Zong* massacre, which concerned the payment of insurance claims for slaves deliberately killed by being thrown overboard by the captain of a slave ship. Lord Mansfield highlighted both the cruelty of the act and a law that considered slaves as property, comparable to horses. The high-profile case went a long way toward turning public opinion against the slave trade.

When Lord Mansfield died in 1793, it was hardly surprising that he left Dido a decent allowance in his will, but that he felt compelled to add that she had honored him with uninterrupted confidence and friendship raised a few eyebrows. He was also careful to state, lest there be any doubt as to her status after his death, that "I confirm to Dido Elizabeth Belle her Freedom."

I continue to visit Leopoldina regularly over the next few months. When the weather is nice, we sit outside in her backyard and eat lunch under the orange trees. These lunches go on into the late afternoon if she warms up and the stories begin to flow. We eat simple salads—lettuce, tomatoes, sesame seeds, and fresh herbs—sometimes accompanied by grilled fish she buys at the market: sardines, sea bass, bream. Her niece and her niece's husband occasionally join us, along with their baby boy, and they bring a cake or ice cream, always vanilla or chocolate, Leopoldina's favorite flavors. Then after eating, over cups of green tea that she takes without any sugar, she asks me how my work is going—since returning to Portugal, I've taken up journalism again and am working at a magazine. We discuss the news, Portuguese and international current affairs, though these things clearly interest her less and less. I tell her about how much journalism has changed while I've been away, how newspaper and magazine newsrooms are no longer the schools of life they once were, with youngsters rubbing shoulders with seasoned old pros. The digital world isn't just speeding up the news process, I tell her, but destroying the transfer of knowledge between generations. She listens to me attentively, but she's mostly being polite, biding her time before we get on to her favorite subjects: my mother; my grandmother; my relatives in the United States, Brazil, and the Netherlands . . .

I'm back living at my mother's again, in my old teenage bedroom. She's lived on her own since divorcing my stepfather, so I know something of what it's like for Leopoldina to live alone. My brothers and sisters have their own homes and families and visit my mother on weekends when they can. My coming back to Portugal, therefore, represents a new phase in all our lives. But as I explain to Leopoldina, I'm not in a hurry to do things. I'm not looking to start a new relationship, for example, or do anything that might require me to make too many personal plans. That said, when we leave home, we children never imagine that we might come back to the same bed and bedroom one day, so while it's nice to be there for my mum, there are mixed emotions. "Well, I'll be glad to have your company for as long as it lasts," says Leopoldina.

One day I tell her about how I financed my student years by playing as a professional musician. "Really?" she says, with a delighted look on her face. I tell her about all the bars I gigged in, the bands I belonged to, the weddings, christenings, and other private parties I performed at where we had to wear black tie and prepare boleros and jazz standards. She enjoys hearing about drunken wedding couples and their strange musical requests, grooms who took up the microphone to impersonate Elvis Presley or Julio Iglesias.

"What about your Portuguese father?" she asks me one day. "Didn't you ever meet him?"

His name is Manuel, I say. He worked as a truck driver. He went to Cape Verde on a work contract, and when that contract ended, he went back to Portugal with the rest of the company's staff. I was age two at the time. But the contract wasn't the only reason he went back; he had a wife and three children living in the north of Portugal. My mum knew this all along but didn't care. Maybe deep down she hoped he might stay with us. But that would have meant hoping that his wife and other children suffered, and my mum never wanted to be happy at someone else's expense.

"Did he stay in touch?" Leopoldina asks.

He sent us a monthly allowance for a while. Then apparently his wife intercepted one of my mum's letters and put a stop to it.

We later heard he and his family moved to France, which is where he'd have been when we ourselves moved to Portugal in 1970. Then in 1977, when I was thirteen, my mum told our family story to some neighbors in the building. They had a car, a 1960 Ford Taunus, and offered to drive us north in the summer. My mum was still in touch with one of my dad's friends, a work colleague from the Cape Verde days, and he told her that, like most Portuguese emigrants, my dad came back to Portugal every August for the summer holidays. So up we went. The house they lived in was out in the middle of the countryside. I stayed in the car with my mum while our neighbors went to investigate. We saw them coming back down a dirt road accompanied by a middle-aged man and a woman dressed in black. My mum got out and spoke to him. He didn't say a word, but he kept his eyes fixed on me. My mum told me to get out. "This is your son, I've brought him here to meet his dad," she said. "How can you be certain he's my husband's child?" asked the woman in black. My mum took my cap off and held up my chin. "That should settle it," she said.

The whole episode lasted no more than ten minutes. We got back in the car and were about to pull away, when my dad came up to the window and asked us where we lived. My mum wrote our address down on a piece of paper and handed it to him. Then we drove off, my dad and his wife getting smaller and smaller in the distance. I spent the whole journey back thinking about how I now had two dads. I wondered whether I ought to mention this trip to my stepfather when he got back from Germany in the winter.

"And did your dad contact you after that?" asks Leopoldina.

No, I say. But I did see him again. Ten years later the band I was in played the summer season of village festivals in northern Portugal. On our way back south, we stopped off to eat somewhere and I bumped into him in a café. We were both stunned at the coincidence. We chatted for a bit, the usual banalities, more me doing the talking than him, telling him about my mum and so on. I remember the look of surprise on his face when I told him I was a musician. He smiled but looked almost ashamed. He must have been about fifty-seven at the time. He was wearing a beret, as country folk typically did in Portugal. This was before mobile phones, so we didn't take a photo together or anything. One of my fellow musicians said afterward that looking at my dad was like looking at me thirty years into the future. But it was a strange encounter. My mum said he was never much of a talker, but the fact was we had nothing much to say to each other. We were perfect strangers. Two people who had nothing in common but blood and a striking physical resemblance.

And so it was, I tell Leopoldina, that I came to have these two father figures: one the memory of a typical Portuguese man from the countryside, humble and reserved, a devout Catholic with a beret and a slightly hunched back, and the other a gregarious Cape Verdean sailor-cook-pirate-adventurer type who spoke smatterings of German, Japanese, Dutch, and Spanish and knew every major port on the planet. I sometimes imagined what it would be like for the two of them to meet. But it seemed like the most unlikely thing in the world to me, like a hurricane encountering a still lake.

One afternoon I get an urgent phone call: Leopoldina is in the hospital. She's unable to speak, someone from the hospital explains—a stroke.

When I visit, I ask her what she's been thinking about.

"I miss our chats and our walks," she writes, "and every night I dream of São Romão, my village." Through her shaky handwriting, I'm transported to the community oven, where the women gathered to bake bread and talk; I'm introduced to the travelers who stopped as they passed through the village, to the Gypsies, farmers, and peddlers, with their horses and donkeys, their black humor and their disdain for life's trials and tribulations. Leopoldina describes her grandfather sitting on a bench in the sun. Her words come slowly, emerging from the nib of the pen, but she tells me she remembers the warm feeling she got when she lay down at night, the light from the oil lamp and the shadows of the adults dancing on the wall, her father getting home from work on his bike, her mother making supper.

I watch her recalling the happy innocence of youth, a joyful ray of light traveling through time and illuminating the hospital room, turning it into a timeless space. She seems to be experiencing that great pleasure that sometimes comes from remembering things, absorbing nostalgia like steam and feeling it spread freshness through the veins. It is the past brought forward for us to experience in the present, but wrapped up in fantasy, free of unhappy memories and worldly imperfections.

Her dull eyes fill up with silent emotion as she describes honeysuckle, roses, and wild orchids blooming on the hill above the village in springtime, their perfume, their exuberance; her and her sisters running barefoot along the walls of the rice fields, the croak of frogs, the splash of snakes fleeing into the water; climbing trees to pick and eat fruit, the smell of watermelons, the sound of the quarreling seasonal rice workers. A whole host of characters calmly enter the room and wander around before us.

I think that her very existence is crystallizing in her shaky handwriting, becoming poetry, beautiful flowers plucked from the heart.

"Do you like birds?"

Leopoldina writes that her cousins and other boys from the village would go looking for nests, losing themselves in the fields and their own private worlds. It's the epitome of the countryside idyll, a shelter from and resistance against hardship, described from a position of peace and distance. Leopoldina has heard that some species of bird that had been on the verge of extinction have now returned to the village heath.

When she tires of writing, we carry on for a while using looks, gestures, and our own imaginations. As she peers into deep waters, the wrinkles at the corners of her mouth, on her forehead, and under her eyes crease; her face is serene and proud. She picks up the pen again and writes that it's a shame she can't be buried in São Romão; the cemetery there closed years ago.

These words make me realize just how much of her life has been spent, that few joys remain for her, and she knows it. I think of her village as a corner of the universe and about time deferred, about permanence and eternity, about all the moments that contribute to a life. I feel an indelible longing for the Sado valley, a nostalgia for heaths, woodland, and rice fields that I've never seen.

She starts writing again: "Will you go there for me . . . ?"

THREE

And before I know it, I'm on a bus leaving Setúbal bound for Alcácer do Sal, ninety kilometers south of Lisbon, the nearest major town to São Romão. Leopoldina's family history has awoken my curiosity, and I haven't been able to stop thinking about the presence of Africans in such a remote and unlikely region. Maybe it's mere journalistic interest. It would certainly make for a more engaging feature than the usual fare the magazine has me churn out. But no, it's more than that. Something about the saga speaks to me very personally. I sense there's more to be discovered, things that Leopoldina has only hinted at that I must see for myself.

The highway splices through Gâmbia, an area of mournful cork oaks and stone pines. I look out the window with growing anxiety, unsure of where to get off. When the mysterious urge takes me, I ring the bell. The bus spits me out, and I set off on foot.

After an hour or so, the immense span of marshland and rice fields spreads out before me. I climb up a hillside of cork trees and look out over the Rio Sado. I see a wooden pontoon and an abandoned house on the riverbank in the distance. In the foreground lie the ruins of a Phoenician trading post, built over two thousand years ago. There's a map on a post, its colors faded, marking the location of ancient ovens and rooms that once corresponded to moldering walls half hidden in the tall grass.

The Sado estuary stretches out as far as the eye can see and looks much as it would have done when the Phoenicians first came in the sixth century BC, sailing in on trireme to explore an obscure corner of Europe.

I press on and come across a village called Monte Velho (Old Hill), which is utterly deserted, as if evacuated in some planned operation. I reach a train track and walk the old wooden gangway that runs alongside it. The driver of a goods train toots furiously when he sees me coming around a corner. I wave in acknowledgment, but he barely looks at me, his eyes fixed straight ahead, his face at once startled by the close encounter and regal inside his orange cabin. When the last freight car passes, I cross the line and slip in between some pine trees.

Rain from recent days has burrowed small, perfectly symmetrical holes in the ground. The earth is moist, and the soil is so fine it disintegrates in my fingers. Walking becomes harder. I join a dirt path that heads down the hill and notice old car tracks disappearing into the undergrowth. The bottoms of my trousers turn dark, wet from the dew in the grass. Sparrows, blackbirds, and chaffinches flee into the trees when they hear me coming. There are no settlements anywhere on the train line between Monte Novo (New Hill) and Alcácer do Sal, and the only inhabited houses I see are on the other side of the track, built into the hillside beyond the last rice fields. Sporadic white farmhouses emerge, with big barns and cow sheds surrounded by cork trees, each individual holding linked to the next by a dirt track.

The air is fresh and full of the sound of chirping birds. After a few hundred yards, the river appears beside me, surging out excitedly from between two small hills, each thick with green cork trees. The morning mist lends the scene a sense of mystery and gives the river surface the look of a steamed-up bathroom mirror. Downstream, the highway crosses the river and the mudflats over a concrete bridge, its three arches poking through the mist to the backdrop of a leaden sky. The track I'm following becomes an ancient footpath, barely visible in the grass. Up ahead the wood opens out onto the rice fields, waterlogged from recent rain.

I look at the birds with Leopoldina's descriptions fresh in my mind, a childhood secret of sorts now shared. But the fact of the matter is I've never been particularly interested in ornithology. I walk along with a pair of binoculars around my neck and a notebook in hand, ready to jot down the markings of whatever I see: size and shape, color of beak, breast, and plumage—anything I might relay to Leopoldina. I listen carefully and walk along looking up into the treetops, then down to the ground, under bushes, in puddles, up to the sky again, hoping to glimpse a blue tit, a tree creeper, a pintail, or, who knows, something even rarer. I move farther and farther away from the river, following the trail of birdsong, but my bird-watching skills prove nonexistent. I put my binoculars and notebook away, but still stop from time to time to enjoy standing silently under the trees.

The Alcácer do Sal train station looks like a scene from Chernobyl. Even the most active imagination would struggle to bring it back to life: people coming and going, faces at train windows, fond farewells on the platform. The toilets still say HOMENS and MULHERES, but they're closed up. A water tank towers over the tracks, heavy with coldness but presumably empty.

Passenger trains stopped calling here a long time ago, so I'm surprised to see a couple of teenage boys wandering along the platform. One of them talks into the ear of the other, who holds him close as they walk. A goods train slowly enters the approach to the station, and the boys stop. When I get closer, I see that one of them is blind and his friend is describing the movement of the train to him, counting out the number of cars. The train makes a deafening noise when it finally comes to a halt, occupying the track from beyond the station buildings to around a bend in the approach, like some mythological beast. The sun is setting, and the lad providing the commentary raises a hand to shield his eyes. Then the blind boy rests a hand on his friend's shoulder, and they walk to the end of the platform and down onto the track.

I walk for ten minutes along the main road into the center of town and am immediately struck by a sense of melancholic dignity. With an abandoned train station and a highway bypass, Alcácer do Sal is in many ways cut off and trapped. But there's something alluring and hospitable about the place too, as if its shadowy streets guard ancient secrets. The castle on the hill, the *al-qasr* ("the castle" in Arabic) that gives the town its name (along with *sal*, the Portuguese word for "salt"), watches over the floodplains, vast and lushly green, and looks down on the white town that climbs the slope from the river. The place has been the scene of historical battles, invasions, clashes between great empires and civilizations, and this knowledge undercuts the sleepiness with a sense of import. In many ways it's the same wetlands hub Leopoldina used to visit as a child for the São João festivities.*

I pass through the town square and come across the library, housed in an eighteenth-century palace, with stone steps and blue-tiled walls surrounding a courtyard. Next door, a two-story town house is undergoing renovation. African workers with vacant expressions on their faces operate a cement mixer.

There's a bar with a terrace, and I collapse into a seat like a sack of potatoes, my body grumbling about the exertion I've unexpectedly forced on it. I order a beer and watch two fluffy clouds break apart reluctantly in the sunset, like a mother and child on the first day of school. On the other side of the road, the Sado flows by silently, with a sadness I detect in all rivers that were once busy with traffic but are now rarely used. I sense the wish to tell us something, to remind us of its worth and possibilities. Meanwhile, buses marked RODOVIÁRIA cross the highway bridge heading south, and a gang of agitated seagulls does likewise. On the horizon, a stork builds a nest atop an old chimney stack.

There's a newspaper on the next table, and I pick it up and read about a dog's skeleton, recently unearthed in the city surrounds, that's been dated to 7,600 years ago, making it the oldest in southern Europe. The skeleton was found in a tomb during excavations of a Mesolithic shell bed, with the dating performed by specialists from Oxford University. Apparently, the diet of a local dog back then featured proteins of marine origin, indicating not only that the dog's owner ate a lot of seafood, but that five thousand years before Christ, man and canine were already companions, sharing if not the same fears, then at least the same joys of seaside living.

Seafood, meat, or fish. Some things never change, and thoughts of prehistoric gastronomy make my tummy rumble. I take a room in the Residencial Cegonha and head out to find something to eat. A board outside O Poço announces cuttlefish stew, so I go in and sit down. There are two young women at another table, foreign tourists I presume.

I take out my notebook, determined to gather my thoughts with the landscape still fresh in my mind, the day's dust on my shoes, and the miles throbbing in my legs. I jot down my impressions to share with Leopoldina, aware of the dangers of embellishment when a journey moves from memory to page. The longer a bend in the river is left to nestle, the more likely it is to assume some dubious symbolism. In our quest for structure, we often make nails of our words and use them to hammer together some argument, no matter how top-heavy it might be with questions rather than answers.

But before I can get too carried away, a gentleman in a dark suit appears and, with due courtesy and old-fashioned manners, strikes up a conversation with the tourists. His is the rusty English of the former immigrant, but it's enough to get across a few insignificant points and to let it be known that he worked for many years in a fish factory in Newfoundland, Canada. They're Dutch, the women tell him, with guarded friendliness, and they're traveling together through Portugal. On the wall above them is a giant poster of Cristiano Ronaldo, grinning from ear to ear and holding a trophy. The man points up and says he's the best soccer player in the world, then adds that he's the most expensive player ever too. The conversation trails off, but the man gets the tourists' attention again when he tells them that Alcácer do Sal was called Salacia Imperatoria Urbs by the Romans. He proceeds to paint a slightly over-the-top picture of the area's import at the time.

"It was a salt region, oh, yes, very rich city with many salt mines."

Would the man know about Gaius Appuleius Diocles, who was the Cristiano Ronaldo of the Roman era? Born in Lamecum (now Lamego) in northern Portugal, Diocles honed his chariot-racing skills at Miróbriga, just south of Alcácer do Sal, which had the largest hippodrome in Lusitania. Indeed, it's said that, after he'd become champion of Hispania at the age of sixteen, it was the rich salt merchants of Salacia Imperatoria Urbs who sponsored his journey to Rome, capital of the empire and the sport.

The Circus Maximus in Rome regularly drew crowds of 250,000, hordes of spectators and a retinue of accompanying bookies, loan sharks, prostitutes, and thieves. Pre-race entertainment included the decapitation and disemboweling of slaves, then the track would be cleared and the trumpets would sound to announce the coming of the chariots and their horses. Diocles favored African horses, said to be faster and more enduring, and believed himself to be the best rider of them. The claim would seem to be borne out by his 1,463 race victories. Some riders won more races than him, but Diocles specifically targeted the more prestigious contests, those that offered the biggest purse. It's estimated that his career earnings make him, in relative terms, the wealthiest athlete in history.

The other remarkable thing about Diocles is that he raced until he was forty-two years old. Chariot racing was supremely dangerous, and most riders died on the track in their early twenties. Diocles outlived them all, though he never made it back to Lusitania to thank his Salacia patrons.

With night descended, I head down to the river to walk off my cuttlefish stew. I pause to look at the water for a moment, and it occurs to me that a moment used to be a measure of time, forty to the solar hour, but has become something rather more fluid, the same way that modern scientists like to think of time as a river. I think about time and the way things happen in it, events and states, as I contemplate the white city reflected in the darkened Rio

Sado. The Romans would have seen much the same reflection, but in the Calipus river; the Arabs as well, only in the Nahr Būdānis. Changes in name that speak of events and states too big for us to grasp. A metamorphosis of miscegenation and civilizations, as Leopoldina would say.

II

Like a long-lost pilgrim, I return to the Lisbon neighborhood I first entered almost forty years ago. I linger at junctions, plunge down alleyways, cut through backstreets, cross courtyards; I recall their mysterious names, their even more mysterious shadows.

I remember the parties my stepfather would throw whenever he got back from Germany. He'd invite all his old pals from Cape Verde, men who spent their lives propping up the bars around here, out of work or signed off with some injury or sickness. He would send me out to buy grilled chicken, fries, and beer, and people would come and go from our flat all weekend.

Leaving my mum's house on the outskirts of the city to return here today is a tribute of sorts. I didn't get back to Portugal in time for my stepdad's funeral. Distance and the sudden nature of his death spared me from that particular experience. My mum and siblings took care of everything, my younger brother coordinating the different bureaucratic stages and legal niceties. I'll never know what the wake and funeral were really like. But his death is also like a new start for me, a new life, a new birth, even, for the family.

It feels less like a trip down memory lane than a trial by labyrinth. My sense of disarray grows the more my curiosity is piqued by the neighborhood's new inhabitants. The area's commerce has changed immeasurably in recent years, from shops and restaurants run by Asian immigrants to sophisticated wine and tapas bars run by locals, but catering to tourists.

The mixture of emotions I had upon first coming here flood back: sadness at leaving my life on São Nicolau behind, awe and wonder at crossing an ocean and finding Lisbon to be so bright and full of hills, trepidation upon entering the underbelly of the great metropole where we were to live and I was to grow up. When I get to the street where we once lived, it's like stepping into the antechamber of another dimension. Not quite the past but something else. I feel a version of myself that no longer exists reaching out to me in a blast of hot air. The metallic grind of a passing tram jolts me back further, wiping away any sense of self I might have built up over the years and convincing me that this place provides the truer picture of who I really am.

The crippling anguish I felt as a child was surely excessive, but it reflected the sadness I saw around me. I see it again now in the guillotine windows of the derelict glass factory, the tufts of weeds that sprout from neglected buildings, facades that offer almost human expressions of solitude. I feel it in the cooing of the pigeons on rooftops, a sound that so tormented me as a child; the scratching of seagulls sheltering under gutters; the deafening screams of children in a hidden schoolyard. Back then the pervading sadness seemed to penetrate the walls of our sublet room and dampen the furniture, smolder in the eyes of our septuagenarian twin-sister neighbors, travel through the plumbing, come and go through our wooden back door, enter the bones of pensioners inching up the street, navigate the sharp bend of Rua dos Poiais de São Bento, and seep into the half-light of the photography studio that occupied the corner building. I'm reminded of days that dragged on like the end of a childhood illness: the slap of domino pieces landing on marble tabletops in bars, the thrum of pouring rain, the whoosh of water rushing down curbs and pavements.

Sadness associated with change—of house, place, home, playground, friends—is the hardest to get over. I felt the first pangs the moment I left my island. Looking at the sea before the boat departed was like I was seeing it for the first time. I felt a great sadness spread out before me as far as the eye could see, sadness for everything I was leaving behind and my being powerless to stop it.

I walk on and see the stone-carved Flor da Murta coat of arms on the corner of Rua do Poço dos Negros, the old post office, the shady Travessa dos Mastros, the never-ending incline of Calçada do Combro. I dread a tram coming along, for I know the honk of its horn will send a wave of despondency rushing through me.

At the Santa Catarina viewpoint, I catch sight of the Rio Tejo, sailboats gliding through the water, ferries flitting over to the other side. Then there is the stone arch over Rua do Alecrim and the smell of medicine coming from the Red Cross post at Praça do Comércio—all of it fills me with sadness. I look at the old streetlamps, the metal plaque outside a school—BOYS' PRIMARY SCHOOL NO. 2, FREE INSTRUCTION—on Rua das Gaivotas, an ice-cream salesman struggling up the hill, three stone steps that lead up to a front door, glimpses of hallways and wooden staircases, sun-kissed yards, clothes drying on balconies, stained-glass panels in doors, dormer windows like cubbyholes on old ships, tiled religious images above doors, the sweeping stone steps of the parliament building, its rigid guards, their elegant uniforms and their white gloves; it all feels so somber to me.

I watch people coming and going, striking out purposefully across the city, full of ideas and dreams appropriate to the age in which they live. I'm walking the streets I knew as a child, the places where my first significant memories were formed, and it's as if these memories look back at me suspiciously, at odds with the man I am now. How much of that boy is still in me? In lockstep with the unstoppable march of time and the infinite possibilities of human existence, my boyhood self and I are both present now: the one who emigrated and his double, the one who forever stayed behind.

For a long time I've fed on a fiction of dividing myself in two, like a cell that split when the moment came to depart. Two possible lives, two different outcomes: different joys, misfortunes, loves, and tragedies. By coming here, I've made these two men stand face-to-face, and I share Spencer Brydon's anguish in Henry James's short story "The Jolly Corner": at night Brydon is pursued by his alter ego, the ghost of the man he might have been, chasing him through the corridors of his old house.

Here I am, the middle-aged man I've become; and there I am, the boy who prowls these streets, who chases after the tram in his plastic flip-flops, energized by the bright summer days, unable to contemplate ever being transformed into a man. I feel removed from the world around me, as if I've stepped back in time, or as if I'm hallucinating banal scenes of everyday life, but with people in cafés staring at me because they recognize me.

They don't. I stop for a brief chat with the owner of a bookstore on Rua do Poço dos Negros, then wander the bars and cake shops, order a coffee here, a bottle of water there. I pay careful attention to my surroundings, eavesdrop on conversations, study gestures. I wonder if what I'm experiencing is some kind of existential crisis or a form of neurosis caused by nostalgia for a lost world. I wonder if it might even be healthy: whether my being unhappy as a child was the consequence of my inability to properly remember São Nicolau, the island where I took my first steps, or our old house on the coast; maybe the melancholy I'm feeling now is just my memory flexing its muscles, performing a little inventory to make sure nothing so self-destructive happens again.

Because this is where it all started. My new life, and with a stepfather to boot; a Cape Verdean family turning, bit by bit, into a Portuguese one. "New Portuguese," as people like us were called, and if ours was a vague and obscure kind of Portugueseness, it nevertheless afforded us the illusion that our migratory adventure was a successful one. But ultimately it is not the world that changes. We do.

FOUR

And as I leave Alcácer do Sal early the next morning, marching along the main road out of town and following signs for Torrão, I get to thinking about Panasco and Domingos, and how the opportunity for these Black men to distinguish themselves came through war. I'm reminded of two other dark-skinned generals, and, as the road cuts through undulating green hills covered in mist, I picture Abraham Petrovitch Gannibal looking out over his estate in the Russian steppe. Gannibal, seized as a child in Africa and enslaved in Constantinople (now Istanbul), ended his life as a Russian nobleman who owned vast tracts of land and, with it, hundreds of serfs. His story is incredible, but for a long time he was principally known in relation to someone else, for he was the great-grandfather of Alexander Pushkin, Russia's most celebrated poet. Pushkin himself wrote a rather embellished account of his great-grandfather's life in *The Arap of Peter the Great*, but a more recent biography by Hugh Barnes, entitled *Gannibal: The Moor of Petersburg*, provides a more faithful portrayal and brings Gannibal back to life in his own right.

I imagine the snow falling in Russia as Gannibal, now in old age, sits down by the fire to be read to by two servants, twin girls from a nearby village whom he has taught to read. Perhaps they remind him of himself and his brother, Abdul, who as boys served Turkish sultans before being sent to Moscow as a gift to Peter the Great. Smarter and more charismatic than his brother, Gannibal found immediate favor with the czar, who made sure he got a good education. Whatever became of poor Abdul? Was there only enough room for one African curiosity in the emperor's household?

Gannibal knew that he'd served as a symbol to the czar, for if even a lowly Black slave could be educated, there was no reason Russia couldn't be modernized. But he hadn't been aware of this as an adolescent, traipsing around various battlefields as Peter the Great's valet. He proved himself a good soldier, brave and quick to grasp military strategy, and became the czar's protégé, adopted as a godson and favored over Tsarevich Alexei, the czar's actual son, who showed no aptitude for military matters. When the czar went to Paris to visit Louis XV, it was Gannibal he took with him. Gannibal was soon discussing differential calculus with Leibniz and philosophy with Diderot, Montesquieu, and Voltaire. They called him "the Black star of the Enlightenment," and he was certainly a living challenge to racist attitudes of the time.

When Peter the Great died, Gannibal's fortunes changed. He may have been a polymath, a polyglot, and an outstanding military engineer, but simmering jealousies and shifting court loyalties saw him banished to Siberia. He was finally brought in from the cold when Peter the Great's second-eldest daughter, Elizabeth, took the throne. He became a prominent member of Elizabeth's court and her most trusted engineer, rising to the rank of major general. After an unhappy first marriage, Gannibal married Christine Regina von Sjöberg, a Swedish-German woman of noble birth, with whom he had ten children, and retired a rich man, having been awarded the Mikhailovsky estate by royal decree.

According to Barnes, Gannibal's years at Mikhailovsky were the happiest of his life, but I nevertheless imagine him living there with a certain wistfulness. It's said he started writing his memoirs but destroyed them, unsatisfied with his efforts. I picture him feeding pages to the fire, content but contemplative, perhaps comparing his fate with that of one of his closest allies in Peter the Great's court, a man named Jan da Costa. Born into a family of Marranos—converted Jews who fled Portugal during the Inquisition—da Costa made his way to Russia via the Netherlands and Hamburg, and he became one of the czar's favorite court jesters. A man of refined manners who had good knowledge of the Scriptures and spoke several languages, it's little wonder he bonded with Gannibal, especially given the outsider status they shared. But considering Peter the Great's declared dislike of Jews, it's somewhat surprising that da Costa became such a prominent figure. He seems to have been another of the czar's pet projects or playthings, and indeed he ended up the butt of one of his jokes, afforded the mock title of King of the Samoyeds and sent to reign over Sommers, an uninhabited sandy island in the Gulf of Finland. At court, he'd been known as the Portuguese Jew Dekosta, and I imagine him telling Gannibal about Portugal and how many Black people there were in Lisbon.

The road snakes left and right, following the course of the river. Rice fields stretch out from both sides, neat and verdant. I wonder if the view here in any way resembles the tobacco and sugarcane plantations of Saint-Domingue, modern-day Haiti, where the other Black general I'd been thinking of grew up.

Thomas-Alexandre Davy de la Pailleterie was born in 1762, the son of a white French aristocrat and a Black concubine. The plantation was a failing business when Thomas-Alexandre's father decided to return to France and claim his inheritance as the Marquis de la Pailleterie. Unable to afford the passage, the future marquis came up with a scheme whereby he sold Thomas-Alexandre to a friend in the French navy and used the proceeds to pay his fare; once in France, he collected his family fortune and bought Thomas-Alexandre back, via the right to redemption, when his friend sailed the boy to France six months later.

After spending his first dozen years on a rustic hillside in the Caribbean, living in a castle in Normandy must have been quite a contrast for Thomas-Alexandre. But that would have been nothing to the Enlightenment Paris he would come to know after his father sold the château and moved them to the Parisian outskirts. In Paris, Thomas-Alexandre would have encountered men like himself, "American Blacks," the products of biracial relationships in colonized parts of the Americas. Many such men wore white wigs and whitened their skin with rice powder, in accordance with the fashion of Louis XV's court.

As Tom Reiss reveals in his Pullitzer Prize–winning book, *The Black Count*, Thomas-Alexandre's father spent lavishly on his son's education. One of the young man's tutors was Chevalier de Saint-Georges, an "American Black" born in Guadaloupe who was a renowned classical musician and a champion fencer. But Thomas-Alexandre's gentleman's lifestyle came to an end when his father remarried and withdrew his son's allowance. Unable to continue his life as a dandy, Thomas-Alexandre joined the army. As a member of the aristocracy, he was entitled to join as an officer, but perhaps fearing that his legitimacy might be called into question, he joined as a private and took to using his mother's name, Dumas.

Private Dumas proved to be a brilliant soldier. He began in the Queen's Dragoons, policing towns to snuff out opposition to the French Revolution, before joining the so-called Légion Noire, a unit of two hundred Black soldiers. There he served as Chevalier de Saint-Georges's second-in-command but soon moved up the ranks in his own right, from brigadier general to division general. This made him commander in chief to ten thousand men, most of them Caucasian.

As a highly rated general, it was only a matter of time before Dumas crossed paths with Napoléon. The two men clashed over Napoléon's laissez-faire attitude toward abuses committed by French soldiers on civilian populations. Perhaps more significantly, Dumas never showed Napoléon the reverence he expected, and he saw through Napoléon's attempts to undermine him.

The two men eventually traveled to Egypt, with Dumas as one of Napoléon's main cavalry commanders. The campaign was a disaster, and Napoléon heard about mutinous talk from Dumas and other generals. Dumas set sail back to France on a galleon out of Alexandria, but several days of stormy weather forced the ship to dock in southern Italy. The Kingdom of Naples was a sworn enemy of the French Revolution, and Dumas was promptly taken hostage. He spent three years imprisoned in Taranto castle, isolated, underfed, and abandoned to his fate by Napoléon.

If his story sounds at all familiar, it's because Thomas-Alexandre Dumas's son, Alexandre Dumas, used it as inspiration for *The Count of Monte Cristo*.

Dumas and Gannibal were both brought to Europe as enslaved boys in the turbulence of the eighteenth century and triumphed in the face of pseudoscientific racism, excelling in the military but also intellectually, only to be conveniently forgotten later. Their life stories were rescued from oblivion by the miracles of literature— eventually by biographers, but initially through works of family fiction. It is truly remarkable that Dumas and Gannibal should both have had such literary titans for descendants, but perhaps their lives and their learning invited it.

The first sunlight of the day sparkles on the water as I cross the bridge into Barrosinha, a sleepy hamlet tucked around the Companhia Agricola farm. I enter the old Sporting Clube da Barrosinha soccer stadium, where long grass and weeds invade the crumbling cement terraces. Clearly a ball hasn't been kicked here for some time. A woman, the only living soul around, digs a hoe into the ground in what must have once been the center circle. When she sees me, she comes over to ask if I'm a tourist. Presumably only a tourist would have any business being here, a forgotten village that passes most people in the blink of an eye as they whizz by on the highway overpass. I climb the terraces at the far side and look out over a serene vista of rice fields and the damp remnants of a recent harvest.

The Sporting Clube and the Companhia Agricola date from the 1940s, when the construction of the Vale do Gaio dam nearby turned the Sado valley into Portugal's main area of rice production. But rice had been cultivated here for a long time before that, since at least the early nineteenth century, in marshland caused by high sea tides and flooding on this, the main branch of the Rio Sado. On a day like today it's hard to imagine waters so high and treacherous that horses sank, dragging men and artillery with them. But the village was also the scene of a notorious battle.

I try to picture the hillsides dotted with people lurking behind blackberry bushes or sheltering under cork trees on the other side of the river. They came from Alcácer do Sal to admire the assembled troops, but ended up witnessing an atrocity they'd speak of until their dying days. But first they raced back to town to tell people to get ready to treat the wounded, to tear up sheets for bandages, gather alcohol, boil water, and prepare makeshift beds.

It's said that more Liberal soldiers died at Barrosinhas than in any other battle in the Portuguese Civil War, which is also known as the War of the Two Brothers, for the two sides rallied around rival siblings' claims to the throne. When Napoléon invaded Portugal in 1807, the Portuguese royal family fled to Brazil. French forces were ultimately driven out of the Iberian Peninsula in 1814, with British help, but rather than return home, the Portuguese royal family stayed in Brazil and Portugal became a British protectorate. By 1820, a group of liberal-minded businessmen had become exasperated by the British presence and established a form of parliament. Portugal's king, Dom Joao VI, returned to Portugal and negotiated a constitutional monarchy with the Liberals, but he faced opposition from his wife, Carlota de Borbón, and their youngest son, Miguel. Religious conservatives, Carlota and Miguel favored an absolutist monarchy. When Dom Joao VI died in 1826, Miguel took charge, promoting Absolutist interests and clashing repeatedly with the Liberals, until civil war broke out in 1828. Pedro, Miguel's elder brother, had remained in Brazil and indeed facilitated Brazil's declaration of independence from Portugal, thus becoming emperor of Brazil. But he now returned, intent on claiming the Portuguese throne and backing the Liberal cause in order to do so.

By late 1833, the Liberals were ascendant, having retaken Lisbon and won control of most major towns and cities, including Setúbal and Alcácer do Sal. Complacency played its part in what happened at Barrosinha, as well as panic and fear. But, perhaps more than anything else, so did the mud.

Liberal troops, on the orders of Lieutenant Colonel Florêncio José da Silva, were positioned in a field at Barrosinha on the morning of November 2, when they were surprised by an attack from Absolutist forces commanded by General José António de Azevedo Lemos. The Absolutist unit comprised fifteen hundred men, most of them on horseback, and the dust and din they produced as they advanced were enough to spook the Liberal forces, far inferior in number and featuring a front line of Portuguese and English marines, but made up primarily of volunteers. Upon seeing the cavalry charge, the volunteers fired their guns in the air and ran for it, only to get stuck in the quagmire of the marshes. The Absolutists soon caught up with them and so began the slaughter. Those who could dropped their weapons and jumped into the Sado to escape, some reaching boats, some swimming to safety, others drowning. Hundreds of Liberals were killed and hundreds more taken prisoner, including Florêncio José da Silva himself, who managed to bargain and bribe his way to freedom before his captors realized who he was. Other officers were not so lucky, as we shall see.

For General Lemos, it was a resounding victory, one that would see him promoted to the rank of lieutenant general and recommended for an Order of Christ medal. That night, he organized a celebratory dinner of meat and rice for his men, with enough wine to keep them going until dawn. The next morning, they marched south with 443 Liberal prisoners, bound for Campo Maior. They hadn't gone far when two Absolutist guerrilla fighters arrived on horseback and talked Lemos into a change of plan. The officers among the Liberal prisoners were promptly separated from their comrades, and six Absolutist riflemen were brought forward. Four other Absolutist soldiers were given spades and told to dig a big hole. One of them was Domingos, Leopoldina's great-great-grandfather.

I leave Barrosinha, walking away from the Sado through fields where a few heads of cattle graze among cork trees. Eventually my path rejoins the road from Alcácer do Sal to Torrão, and I walk for the best part of an hour before I reach my destination: the Herdade de Algalé estate. Its gates, alas, are firmly closed.

Then I notice a piece of paper stuck to a blue-and-white cement wall. "All matters concerning these three properties should be dealt with by calling . . ." I ring the number. A man with an authoritative voice answers, and I explain why I'm here. "Yes, there was a massacre here," he says with a sigh. "I'm going to have to start charging visitors at this rate, or get the town hall to help pay for the upkeep. But sure, wait where you are, I'll try to find someone to come and get you."

Gil is a tall, bald Alentejano man in a hurry. Our Jeep speeds past clusters of cork and pine trees, old stone houses, and barns that now accommodate heavy machinery and tractors. We go down a ravine where building work is under way on a new irrigation channel, then cut back on ourselves and move toward a herd of cows. The cows get to their feet and run off ahead of us, flustered, rounding up their calves. We stop for Gil to get out and open a gate in the fence, and then suddenly there it is, an obelisk among the cow pats.

The field is flanked on one side by a hill of oak and chestnut trees that give the monument a ghostly sort of honor guard. The obelisk looks to be about ten feet tall and sits in a modest flower bed marked off by four wooden stakes and a wire fence. "To stop the cows from eating the plants," Gil explains. There's no bench or plaque, just the solitary stone obelisk standing in a field, silently seeking justice or symbolizing the futility of war.

Carved into the stone on two sides is an account of what happened: TWENTY-NINE OFFICERS LOYAL TO THE CROWN, HELD PRISONER BY USURPER TROOPS AFTER THE BATTLE OF ALCÁCER, WERE BARBAROUSLY EXECUTED HERE ON THE FOURTH DAY OF THE MONTH OF NOVEMBER, 1833.

The officers were brought out in groups of four and shot by the six-man firing squad. As the dead men fell into the hole dug for their communal grave, guns were reloaded and the next four prisoners led out. It was a scene that Leopoldina had heard described by her grandmother Eugénia, who'd heard it from Zulmira, who'd heard it from Josefa, who'd heard it from her husband, Domingos.

Lepoldina liked to think that witnessing the Massacre of Algalé, as it became known, prompted Domingos to desert the Absolutist army. If it did, he nevertheless joined the Absolutist rebels in the aftermath of the civil war. He was not alone. If city people favored the Liberals, support for the Absolutists remained strong among the rural poor, who tended to be more conservative and religious. Two worlds faced off in these fields, with the level of animosity evident in the cruelty of the acts. Two causes: one monarchist and conservative, the other liberal and reformist, both capable of inspiring men to stain an innocent November morning with blood.

Domingos had answered the sitting sovereign's call and rallied to the flag, taken with some sublime notion that he was defending his *pátria*. Yet he was a Black man fighting on the side of tradition, on behalf of the status quo, at a time when there were still enslaved Black people in Portugal. Domingos put his body on the line for the reactionaries when he was the very embodiment of change; no one represented the modern Portuguese man and what a new and unified society might look like more than he did.

It's easy to look back and see a misguided young man driven by fantasy, rebellion, nonconformism, and some romantic belief in the dawn of a new era. He was certainly naive to think he could rise above the limitations imposed on him by his skin color. But we should perhaps give him more credit too, for he was evidently a man of integrity. Doubtless he pursued freedom the way he did in good faith, trusting in his own drive and moral fiber. It's hard to imagine him settling for an Absolutist victory that did not reward him with liberty or that required him to show reverence. He does not seem to have been the sort of man who'd have disappeared into his shell to protect himself or kept his head down to lessen life's hardships. At the humbler end of society, people often develop an awareness of their own idiosyncrasies in such a way that allows them to remain true to themselves and the world as they find it— which in Domingos's case was a world created by God.

On the other two sides of the obelisk, the names of the unfortunate victims are engraved in the stone: Alexandre Ferreira Benfeito, Bento Branco da Paz Braz, António Teno Braz, António Tocinho Chambel, Francisco de Mattos e Silva Paula Botelho, Francisco Manuel Vieira, Francisco de Amado, Francisco Maria do Torno, João José de Andrade, Joaquim de Beja Capucho, João Maria de Oliveira, Lourenço Supando Manuel, José Gomes Martinho, António de Mira, Manuel Joaquim Afonso, Pedro Maria Craruijol . . .

The rest of the names have eroded away. Ravaged by time, wiped from the surface of the stone, they are now definitively dead. It seems like a cruel trick of history, but then history sometimes likes to evoke the perpetual present to remind us that we can't fight the chaos, that even our epoch-defining battles turn to dust.

III

As I stand on Rua do Poço dos Negros, I imagine a strange, invisible thread that connects my first primary school, the second-floor flat in which we lived, and the ground-floor apartment where Andresa do Nascimento became A Preta Fernanda, the most famous African in Lisbon.

There are a number of different versions of her extraordinary life, but all derive from the autobiography she left behind, a somewhat fantastical work in which it's hard to separate fact and fiction, pretense and parody. But it seems safe to say she came from Ribeira da Barca, on Santiago—though she may have first moved to Cape Verde from Guinea-Bissau—and that her parents earned a living as nut gatherers. Whether she really did accompany Portugal's most celebrated novelist, Eça de Queirós, up the steps and into his box seat at the Trinidade Theater is harder to confirm, no matter how gushingly the book describes the episode. Perhaps "it's too good a story not to be true," as Andresa liked to say.

Her book, *Recordações d'uma colonial* (*Recollections of a Colonial Woman*), uses consciously racist language and delights in reinforcing stereotypical notions of the time. It was ghostwritten by two white men but presented as Andresa's own work, albeit under the pen name of Fernanda do Vale, a woman variously described as a wife, lover, and libertine, a model, courtesan, and bullfighter.

She's portrayed as tough, bold, and fearless, a lascivious African woman who kept the company of diplomats, politicians, artists, writers, and journalists and dallied with men such as Fritz Kemps, the German beer manufacturer she married.

She never moved far in Lisbon. When she first arrived in the city on Fritz's arm in 1878, having met him in Senegal, they installed themselves at the Hotel de France on Rua de São Paulo, long before the area became home to numerous Cape Verdean families. When Fritz died, forcing her to fend for herself, she went into service with the Cavalcantis, a Piedmont family living on Rua do Poço dos Negros. There she became acquainted with high society, and when the family eventually left town, she established a bohemian bordello in Bairro Alto. A Preta Fernanda the madam kept a close eye on the girls in her employ, but still found time to discuss the "Futurist Manifesto" with José de Almada Negreiros, a celebrated mixed-race artist from São Tomé and Príncipe.

Her most lasting presence in Lisbon is in Praça Dom Luís, where she is immortalized in sculpture. In 1880, she sat as the model for an artist creating a statue of a Black woman holding a child. Positioned at the foot of a monument honoring the Marquis of Sá da Bandeira, a prime minister who passed antislavery legislation, the figure based on Fernanda sits, broken chains at her ankles, pointing out the marquis's name to the child.

Recordações d'uma colonial recounts in detail how its protagonist falls in love with a ship's captain, the fast-talking Jerónimo Antunes Martins, and elopes with him from Cape Verde to Senegal. Readers are offered a list of the items the captain buys for her in a French fashion store in Dakar: a black tulle hat, a floral silk skirt, a corset, a long-sleeved bodice, several underskirts, and thigh-length lace panties. Prior to this, the book has great fun describing the environment in which Fernanda supposedly grew up, a world of mud huts, ornamental feathers, *ai-iué* chanting, drums, and indigenous clothing—loincloths for the men and straw skirts for the women.

By the time *Recordações d'uma colonial* came out in 1912, Andresa do Nascimento was fifty-three years old and evidently bitter and vindictive enough to furnish her ghostwriters with a list of all the men she'd had in her bed. Jerónimo Martins comes first, followed by Fritz, then a vast array of journalists, officers, captains, sergeants, servants, businessmen, guardsmen, newspaper editors, scribes, solicitors, cadets, and an acrobat named Pissiuti. Each entry is accompanied by a short, cutting commentary on the man's sexual performance.

Rather less salaciously, the book features a charming and quite curious reference to *cachupa* and how to make it. This probably ranks as the first mention of Cape Verde's national dish in any work of literature. While the book is clearly primarily the fanciful work of Andresa's ghostwriters, it does at least seem to have been partially based on conversations with her, which suggests Andresa do Nascimento/Fernanda do Vale/A Preta Fernanda liked to cook and that, in her own small way, she influenced the eating habits of her time. Her recipe for *cachupa* could, in fact, be the most authentic item in the entire "autobiography."

These days you can get *cachupa* on Rua do Poço dos Negros at the Cape Verdean restaurant Tambarina. I don't recall whether the dish was on the menu when my mother married my stepfather, but I do have other memories of that day. The reception was held in our modest flat, and I remember going up to the attic room with a girl wearing white shoes and a ribbon in her hair. We played games in the dark: the damsel in distress, beauty and the beast. Her two big eyes shone bright in the gloom, and I couldn't resist reaching out and touching her curly hair, as thick and impenetrable as a dense forest. I remember adolescent heat rushing up my arms as my hands held her shoulders, the strange fire that seemed to burn inside her, her total submission to my timid advances. I remember or imagine—I'm not entirely sure which—the brief pulsing silence of two beings momentarily absent from the world.

Then I pointed to the strip of light under the door: "Someone's coming . . . Shh." We squeezed our hands together tightly and almost stopped breathing. She said, "Yes, all right . . ." and I noticed the perfect shape of her mouth, the way the words rolled off her tongue as if ready to be eaten.

On the main door to our old building there is now an iron knocker shaped like the back of a young woman's hand, which seems apt. I've returned to a place of youthful innocence and a powerful memory, but I cannot recall the girl's name. All I remember is that she was on her way to Italy from São Nicolau and that the sun was shining that day we split the universe in two.

Am I alone in remembering the special energy of that afternoon in the attic? There's no way of knowing. She held a book in her hand, and if I close my eyes I can see the cover, the color of it, but I can't grasp the title. Ariadne's thread, perhaps, but a memory so insubstantial it could vanish from one moment to the next.

That one of us remembers is enough for the day to have existed, though. Besides, from that tiny morsel of an afternoon, my overactive teenage imagination built an entire love story that fed my nighttime desires for years, filling a void that opened up around me once she'd gone.

Not long after remarrying, my mother replied to an advertisement in the newspaper and went to work for Dona Amélia as a maid. Dona Amélia was a widow in her eighties. She was thickset, with plump arms and glassy eyes. One day I asked her if she'd ever drunk rainwater, and the question so perplexed her that she fled the room without answering, muttering to herself all the way down the corridor.

My afternoons were spent staring at the bare trees on Avenida João Crisóstomo to the doleful soundtrack of the building's cranking wooden elevator. They were slow afternoons, sad, desolate, and infinite. I looked down from the balcony and watched people and cars blending into the paleness of the buildings in the distance. Inside the apartment, the monotonous voices of television or radio presenters, or Dona Amélia issuing my mother instructions, echoed off the walls like the sound in the rooms of a museum.

One summer, we were invited by Dona Amélia to accompany her and her bourgeois family on a short holiday to their country estate outside Lisbon. Traveling in the back of the car, looking out the window, I was mesmerized by the orange light pouring through the trees. I didn't want to go, and I recall feeling sadder than I'd ever felt before, the heaviness of my mood surpassing all previous sadnesses, or replacing those that had passed their expiration date. A few days later and my spirits had revived. I was energized by the long walks in the fields and the never-ending warm summer days. I spent my mornings wandering among orchards, lost for hours until someone called me in for lunch.

Perhaps being in the back seat of the car had reminded me of sitting in the cabin of a ship in the harbor of Porto Grande, São Vicente, as it pushed out into the infinite sea, bound for Portugal. I remember the suffocating heat and the unanswered terror of seeing my native land disappear on the horizon, my world slowly melting away, sucked in between the big blue sky and the vast silver of the sea. My memory of this moment comes with a backdrop of metallic sound: the intense, insistent shudder of the *Amélia de Mello*'s machine room. I was six, accompanied only by a man I didn't yet know.

After five days at sea, in which I recall seeing no land except the vague outline of the Canary Islands, we reached Portugal and I was reunited with my mother. It was a strange reunion amid the hustle and bustle of Lisbon's Alcântara Port Terminal. When I first saw her, it was like coming face-to-face with a vaguely familiar film star.

I went down the steps of the boat holding hands with that peculiar man who would become my stepfather. At the bottom of the steps was a smiling lady dressed in a stripy beige jacket-and-skirt suit, a high-collared brown shirt, and white high-heeled shoes. She was certainly very pretty, this woman, with a simple, bright smile that showed off a neat row of white teeth. When I realized this woman was actually my mother, the joy that flooded through me was such that it was as if I were seeing her for the first time. She came to me, took me by the shoulders, and squeezed me to her chest. Then she opened her bag and took out a rice cake wrapped in a napkin. It was a moment of astonishing relief, a combination of jaunty wonder at the promise of a new world and the pure joy that exists between mother and child. Then it was interrupted by this man. My travel companion approached and gave my mother a gentle kiss on the lips. A fleeting kiss, or a leaning in of the lips, to be more precise. Even I could tell the difference between "they gave each other a kiss" and "they kissed."

In childhood, everything is experienced with the awe of incomprehension. It's fertile ground for those of us with a poetic disposition, the whole world for a muse. There was an American TV series on at the time called *The Courtship of Eddie's Father*, in which the father of a boy of around my age sought to remarry after his wife, the boy's mother, died. The cameras always made sure to capture the father's eyes—and his desperate hope that Eddie would like each prospective stepmother.

That first morning in Portugal I was led to my new room, where I lay on the bed listening to the giggles of my mother and future stepfather coming from across the hall. I remembered how, back on the terrace of the bar on board the *Amélia de Mello*, this man and his friends offered me five crowns if I'd lift up the skirts of women standing chatting at the guardrail.

FIVE

And the Sado slithers sleepily by, like a snake waiting to be woken by the sun. It's thin here, timid of flow and almost entirely shaded by a bank of trees. The reeds at its edges are dry, its bed a shiny black of viscous mud. Rivers slim down for the summer season too, but this one is skeletal, almost moribund.

I stand for a while and watch the drops of dew that dangle on the tips of the reeds, each one a mysterious, scintillating planet. A dark red crayfish comes out of the grass and runs at me with its pincers drawn. What I take to be some kind of desperate, suicidally courageous attack turns out to be the advance party of a Lilliputian army: dozens more crustaceans emerge and march across the road, then disappear into the undergrowth on the other side.

Instead of an assault, the crayfish triggers a memory: the Black history exhibition I'd visited in Cascais alongside, if not quite with, Leopoldina. It was the fact that Black slaves were unbaptized, the exhibition emphasized, that enabled their masters to treat them like animals. Their Portuguese owners raised and sold them as human beasts of burden, making a handsome profit from the trade. Though I'd known this, seeing the shackles and handcuffs, and especially the dog collars and tags—many of which had been collected by José Leite de Vasconcelos, a Portuguese ethnographer—brought home just how extreme this animalization was. "This nigger belongs to Agostinho de Lafetá do Carvalhal of Óbidos . . ."; "This slave belongs to Luís Cardozo de Mello, resident of Benavente . . ."

A red-and-white sign nailed on a tree informs me I'm entering hunting territory. I follow a path that winds into a wood of pine, cork oak, and eucalyptus trees. I come across an irrigation canal before brambles hamper my progress, then barking dogs try to repel me, like the guardians of some virgin pasture. But they're on the other side of the canal, and provided that remains the case, I'm safe.

I pass two sluiceways: one has a metal wheel with several paddles and appears to control the flow and supply of the water; the other, larger and built below ground level, separates the flow of one irrigation canal from another. In some places, the canal is practically dry, while at others, a gentle ripple of water washes over the silt and attracts birds for refreshment. At other points there is enough depth for tiny fish to swim.

I stop to drink from my water bottle and take a sandwich from my rucksack. I'm on higher ground now and can see the river below, slothful and metallic. The only sound I hear is birds chirping in the trees, then the steady rhythm of my footsteps as I set off again, trouser legs brushing through the long grass. Then a path leads me away from the irrigation canal, back toward the river. The valley spreads out before me like a giant yellow-green lake, filled with rice plants waiting to be harvested.

Passing the Herdade de Arouca estate, the sound of a combine harvester reaches me from across the valley. I stand and watch for a while. From a distance, the combine and its accompanying tractor and trailer look like big mammals on the African savanna. The combine moves back and forth in continuous labor, its blades cutting through the stems of the rice plants at ground level and leaving circles in the soil. An alarm sounds every time the driver puts the vehicle into reverse, which disrupts the group of egrets who follow behind the machine like seagulls over a trawler, swooping in to peck at freshly exposed grubs and other treats. The driver parks the combine beside the tractor and maneuvers a tube over the trailer. He flicks a switch and grains of rice start to pour in.

I press on until I reach Porto d'El Rei. The old palace building lost the glass in its windows some time ago, but the walls are sturdy and the masonry remains pristine. Built in a somber Mannerist style, the palace now lies in a pitiful, if tranquil, state of abandon, a symbol of a once-bustling river terminus that reached its own end of the line.

All that remains of the inland port's glory days is a stone arch at the entrance to the old goods yard. Emblazoned with a magnificent coat of arms, it seems oblivious to the surrounding decadence and ruin. Everything else has fallen to the ground or been swamped by wild fig and loquat trees. The stone wharf is almost entirely hidden by an impenetrable tangle of brambles.

There would once have been an island here, in the middle of the river, where boats could unload and turn around. But everything is silted up now, the river reduced to a meander through slush and bush, a footnote in history.

There is a resigned air to the disrepair of the port buildings, a sort of magnanimous acceptance of the damage wrought by progress. It's a scene repeated all over Portugal. This was as far inland as the Sado was navigable and, as such, a dock upon which kings disembarked on the way to their hunting lodges in the Alentejo—Porto d'El Rei means "King's Port" in old Portuguese.

When the first steamboat line linking Alcácer do Sal, Setúbal, and Lisbon opened in 1847, with some services extending all the way to Porto d'El Rei, the place became a hub for transporting regional produce to the capital. But the opening of the Alentejo railroad in 1853 marked the beginning of the end, and a branch line to Setúbal, built in 1861, rendered Alcácer do Sal's granaries obsolete. Porto d'El Rei ceased to welcome either kings or crops.

Leopoldina's great-uncle worked on the steamboats his whole life. Pedro Fogueiro: something of a vagabond, a slippery sailor who really did have a girl in every port. It's said he left as many as ten children spread around the steamboat line's four main calling points: Alcácer do Sal, Setúbal, Sesimbra, and Lisbon. But he never married, and he made his boat his only home.

These were times of great poverty and hunger. Pedro's job would have given him the means and mobility to ensure a great welcome whenever and wherever he called. His charm and manners apparently seemed too good to be true for a simple steamboat stoker: women tended to believe there was more to him than met the eye. And, of course, he wasn't just a steamboat stoker; he had his own clients he did deliveries for, traveling between the four ports doing odd jobs and moving contraband. As the twentieth century dawned, he aligned himself with the republicans, attending meetings in the four towns and spreading pamphlets and news between them.

A lovable rogue, Pedro was also a lively dancer who would have been a regular presence in the region's dance halls and at saint's day parties. He was a fin de siècle mixed-race man who blended a provincial form of belle epoque grace with a dash of *marialvismo*—a Portuguese way of being commonly associated with fado music and old-fashioned masculine values, a love of seedy bars, bullfighting, and fatalism. Pedro apparently rejected every offer of job promotion that came his way and every chance of social advancement. It's no surprise Leopoldina remembers him as an unpredictable man, but one who knew how to play the mandolin. More than anything, he guarded his freedom with religious fervor.

He would likely have been disappointed by Porto d'El Rei now. Picturing a boat anchored here challenges the capacity of my imagination. The old palace and its connecting buildings may still stand to attention, as if waiting for something to happen, but the place is deserted, and you can't even see the river from their doorways anymore. The water still trickles by, but rather than evoke a lost world or keep a secret history alive, it makes the very idea seem fanciful. I close my eyes and try to conjure up the sound of the ships' horns, the cries and whistles of longshoremen and sailors. But all I hear is a stork taking flight after being startled by my presence and the eerie beating of its wings.

For a long time Porto d'El Rei was the last stop for anyone traveling up the Sado. There would have been a fair number of slaves among them, bound for the rice fields. But when a former slave named Samuel got off here in the late eighteenth century, he had other aims in mind.

His incredible story came to light thanks to the abolitionist Thomé Ferreira de Andrade, a young lawyer born in Salvador de Bahia, Brazil, the son of a wealthy Portuguese man with links to the court of King José I. After reading law at the University of Coimbra, Ferreira de Andrade decided to stay on in Portugal and set up a practice in Lisbon. He initially focused on preventing enslaved men and women from being separated from their families and sent to Maranhão, Brazil. Later he became known for representing Black fraternities, Catholic religious orders that used what few state privileges their evangelizing mission afforded them to help slaves defend their rights.

A 1761 law prohibited the import of enslaved Africans to Portugal: anyone entering a Portuguese port with an enslaved person on board was obliged to set that person free. The fraternities organized for commissions to inspect new arrivals, especially ships from Brazil, which often had enslaved men among the crew or as passengers, accompanying their Brazilian masters on trips to Europe. The fraternities engaged lawyers to patrol the Cais da Ribeira docks, demand that papers be presented, and ensure that customs officials granted the enslaved their liberty.

Because the 1761 law prevented new slaves from entering the country but allowed slavery through birth to continue, one notorious consequence was forced procreation: slave owners obliged their slaves to breed in order to sell their children. The fraternities alerted Ferreira de Andrade to the practice, and he publicly denounced it, drawing particular attention to the problem in the Alentejo and the Algarve, where it was more remote and easier for people to evade the law.

Ferreira de Andrade began winning cases and gaining influence in court, but the more success he had, the more enemies he made. He was eventually badly beaten and left for dead, his assailants never identified. He recovered in time to see the Freedom of Wombs Law introduced in 1773, which granted freedom to all newborns and anyone whose enslaved condition could be traced back to their great-grandparents. Forced procreation came to an end.

Ferreira de Andrade's small contribution to the fight against slavery in Portugal was lost to history until his papers were found a century later by the Marquis of Sá da Bandeira, whose statue A Preta Fernanda adorns. Among a cache of legal tracts, plea bargains, and letters Ferreira de Andrade sent to members of the court, there was an altogether different text in the lawyer's hand: "A odisseia do antigo escravo Samuel" ("The Odyssey of the Former Slave Samuel").

In 1773, Samuel worked on a fishing boat in Leça da Palmeira, in the north of Portugal. He, like the boat, was owned by Captain Monteiro Lobato. By then, Samuel had been married to Caetana, a woman he'd met at the São João street party, for over ten years. She'd been born enslaved and sold, at the age of twelve, to a textiles magnate. But she was fond of her owners, especially the mistress, who had raised her almost as a daughter.

When this mistress died, however, Caetana's circumstances changed. The master gradually stepped back from running the family business and handed over the reins to Luis Vieira, his eldest son. Luis Vieira had always disapproved of the goodwill his parents had shown toward Caetana, goodwill that had included allowing her to do something rare among slaves, namely to marry. Caetana's life had nevertheless been one of constant toil, involving endless household chores and running errands to and from the market or the textiles warehouse.

The death of the mistress coincided with Caetana's pregnancy, and in the eyes of Luis Vieira, his parents' indulgence had resulted in yet another mouth to feed. To avoid being a burden, Samuel and Caetana moved, with their newborn son, Salvador, to live in a hut near the textiles outlet in Matosinhos. But Luis Vieira proved to be a hopeless manager and the family business began to fail. Debts mounted, until one day he called Caetana into his study, refused to look her in the eye, and informed her that he'd decided to sell Salvador. He'd struck a deal with a businessman in Lisbon and gotten a good price. The boy had reached the fine age of nine, and it was the only way of paying off the debts that were crippling the family.

Caetana felt the ground open up beneath her feet. She tried everything to persuade Luis Vieira not to sell her child: she promised to work longer hours and said Samuel would do odd jobs in whatever spare time he had to help pay off the debt. Luis Vieira remained unmoved. Caetana went to see the parish priest, who had confirmed and married them, and begged him to intervene. As a last resort, she went to speak to the master himself, but he had distanced himself from family affairs and become lost to drink. Salvador was taken away by his new owner, one José de Sousa Carrilho, just after Christmas.

Sometime later, the priest called Caetana aside after Mass one day and told her about the new law. He knew that she, her mother, and her grandmother had all been slaves, which made Salvador a fourth-generation slave, meaning he was now free. The priest had even checked the parish birth registry: Caetana had been born in Leça da Palmeira to a mother who was herself the daughter of a slave born in Angola and purchased in Lisbon.

Samuel's first thought was to flee immediately and go in search of their son. But this was easier said than done, and he ended up explaining the situation to his owner, Captain Lobato, who agreed to sell him his freedom. The price they agreed on took Samuel five long years to earn. When he was finally free, he set off that very night, equipped with little more than the packed lunch of dried fish and bread that Caetana had made for him.

Samuel walked for days, through mountains, valleys, swamps, fields, and orchards. He slept wherever he found himself as night fell, preferably under a hedge or bush that offered some shelter from the rain, and he avoided towns and villages, so as not to invite trouble. He favored footpaths over roads, to avoid highwaymen. Whenever he came across a river or stream, he checked no one was around, then took a dip to refresh himself.

When he reached Coimbra, having walked eighty miles, he sought out an old Black man named Inácio, who led the town's Black fraternity. Inácio put Samuel up for the night and gave him a hot meal and a bath. While Samuel recovered his strength, Inácio tried to find an address for the Sousa Carrilho family in Lisbon. Samuel resumed his journey the next day, supplied with a list of safe houses and allies he could ask for help between Coimbra and Lisbon.

When he reached Leiria, he had to flee a group of highwaymen who'd seen him paying for supplies with a coin. He hid in a tree and spent the night in its branches before continuing on.

He sometimes met other Black men working in fields or on boats on the rivers. He'd stop to ask them for information: What was the best route to Lisbon? How many days' walk to the next town? But mostly he stayed out of sight and just watched them, and when they'd left and the sun had set, he came out from the trees and dug up a melon or foraged for an apple or orange in an orchard.

At Santarém, he headed for the river docks and touted his services as an experienced sailor and strong ship hand. The captain of a boat transporting wine barrels took him on, and he worked his passage to Lisbon. Two months after leaving Leça da Palmeira, Samuel reached the capital.

He'd never been to Lisbon before and was impressed by the number of people, the sight of sedan chairs and horses in the streets, and the new buildings and town squares, built after the 1755 earthquake. He made his way to the convent in the neighborhood of Graça, where Inácio had told him to seek out a particular man in the Black fraternity. When Samuel reached the convent, he was told the man in question was sick, but was asked for his story and told to come back in two weeks. He headed back to the Ribeira das Naus docks and found work. But when he went back to the convent, he was informed that the Sousa Carrilho family had left Lisbon and moved to Faro three years ago.

Faro is a town on the south coast in the eastern Algarve, 150 miles away from Lisbon. Samuel tried to get a post as a deckhand on boats bound for the Algarve, but the best he could manage was a sailboat that ran the goods route to Alcácer do Sal. He disembarked at Porto d'El Rei in the early spring.

He set off walking again, passing through Torrão and then back into the fields, traversing valleys, skirting villages, crossing streams, determined to fulfill his promise to Caetana. He saw other Black people traveling with their owners, but also met slaves out on their own, running some errand to the next town. He walked and talked with some of them for hours, each and every one amazed at his courage and determination.

He reached Ferreira do Alentejo just as the town's Our Lady of the Rosary festival was getting under way. The Black fraternities had adopted Our Lady of the Rosary as their patron saint, and Samuel joined in the celebrations with other Black worshippers. He found himself in São Brás de Alportel on Easter Sunday, and his heart rejoiced at the magnificence of the parade: the flower-lined streets and rousing hallelujahs surely indicated that he'd found the path to paradise; it could only be a good omen.

Indeed, he soon reached Faro, and it wasn't difficult to find the Sousa Carrilho estate a few miles west of the city walls. He entered the property and explained why he'd come, but was told the master had gone to Tavira for the day and wouldn't be back until nightfall. Samuel said he'd come back the next day, but first he took a look around the farm, asking after a young Black lad named Salvador. The boy had apparently accompanied the master, as he always did.

The next morning, Samuel returned and went up to the house. When asked on whose behalf he'd come, he said, "On my own behalf." While he waited at the bottom of the steps, he saw a Black boy lead a horse out of the stable. José de Sousa Carrilho appeared at the door that very moment. He looked Samuel up and down with evident disdain and asked him what he wanted. Samuel took off his hat and explained who he was and where he'd come from. Then he said:

"I believe sir has a Black lad by the name of Salvador, bought in Matosinhos."

"So what?"

"Well, sir, the boy is the son the Good Lord chose to give to me and Caetana, my wife, and according to the new royal decree, the boy is now free."

Having noticed that Sousa Carrilho's wife had approached, as well as several curious farmhands, Samuel raised his voice so that his words could be heard by all.

"I have letters here, sir, signed by the parish priest of Matosinhos, that prove what I say is true. Salvador is a free man."

Sousa Carrilho looked at his wife and the others who'd assembled. He walked down a few steps and took the papers from Samuel's hand. He glanced over them, a look of skepticism on his face, and then threw them on the ground.

"I bought him, he's mine," he said. "If you want him, you'll have to pay me the same amount I paid for him, which I very much doubt a man in your position can afford."

The boy with the horse watched on in silence, his hands gripping ever tighter to the reins. Then Sousa Carrilho ordered him inside, before going in himself, shutting the door firmly behind him.

Samuel had been told to expect such difficulties. He went back into Faro and reported to the local Black fraternity, who told him to go and see a friendly lawyer who happened to be in town. Thomé Ferreira de Andrade welcomed Samuel into the room he'd taken in a local inn, listened to his story, and examined the priest's letters under candlelight. Then he drafted a missive and had it dispatched immediately to Sousa Carrilho. It gave Sousa Carrilho two days to grant Salvador his liberty or face being hauled before the local magistrate.

Three days later, young Salvador appeared at Ferreira de Andrade's door with a bundle on his back. Samuel and Salvador sailed to Lisbon on the same boat as Ferreira de Andrade a few days later, their tickets paid for by the Black fraternity. Ferreira de Andrade made the most of the journey to get the story of Samuel's odyssey down on paper.

IV

He called it Bicho, a Portuguese word meaning "animal," but he loved it like a child. He was particularly affectionate toward it when drunk, cradling it in his arms as he walked around the house. Though everyone called it a turtle, it was actually a tortoise, and, like all tortoises, it was slow moving and spent long stretches of the year in hibernation. Hidden in the house somewhere, it was forgotten by everyone until there was a sound like a persistent tapping, and we'd find it awake again, stuck behind the sofa or the wardrobe. Before it moved in with us, Bicho had been my stepfather's loyal companion and accompanied him on sea voyages all over the world. It became our longest-lasting pet, until one day we found it dead, jammed between the wall and an old armchair.

So many memories come flooding back to me while I'm living at my mother's house.

My younger brother eventually joined us in Lisbon, and, like most families with kids, the prospect of more space for less money farther out proved irresistible. We moved away from São Bento and out to the eastern suburbs. My first discovery was that the decrepitude I knew from the inner city was still present in the outskirts, it just expressed itself differently. The quiet, dull miserableness of the old town made way for brighter colors and constant noise in the new-build areas. People's faces were still sad, but in a different way. In the old town they were wrinkled and weathered, as if weighed down by the history right there on their doorstep, the city's unchanging landscape. In the periphery, despite considerable amounts of open space, faces looked longer, angrier, and more desperate.

Being so far removed from the city's center, which was an hour away on a bumpy single-decker bus, brought out a sense of provincial anonymity and semiwild abandon in suburban inhabitants. These were, of course, embedded characteristics carried forward from previous generations who had brought them with them when they first migrated to the capital from rural Alentejo or Beira.

Still, my childhood sadness, feeding as it did off anything that appeared old, slow, ruined, or incomplete, began to lift. The open spaces, the wasteland, the mysterious country lanes, the solitary trees, and the birdsong that seemed to call to me impatiently— all of it filled me with, if not joy, then a warm sort of pastoral melancholy.

Staying in my old bedroom, I come across old books and remember the epic adolescent love stories that played out within these four walls. The sound of the rain on the roof tiles, the wind whistling at the window, the smell of damp; these things are highly evocative, but I can just as easily be swept up by memories of more trivial things: an old stamp, a crooked floor tile, an empty chair. At night I wander the dark, empty house—the silent furniture, the orphaned plants, the pictures trying to escape from the walls— and sense the shadows of my own family trying to sneak away and abandon me.

My mother drags herself around the house, from the living room to the kitchen, from her bedroom to the bathroom, like someone searching for a door to a different era. The wooden stairs creak in condescending nostalgia for a bygone age. She lives alone now, with only Brazilian and Portuguese soap opera actors for company. Her words seem to be on the verge of extinction through lack of use, the telephone her periscope to the surface.

After dinner we sit in the lounge and listen to old music from the islands. She shares a few stories about the house we had on São Nicolau, the men and women who would come down from farther up the valley and call in for a glass of fresh water and a bit of conversation. We've moved forward in time, but it's as though nothing has changed, as if these people might walk through the door at any moment and fill the house with the excitement of carnival. It is, I guess, her gentle way of subverting our linear human timeline.

The personal things my mother keeps are mere decorative items, but the years have afforded them a status approaching kinship: an ancient chair, a standing ashtray, a cutlery set from a TAP flight, a yet-to-be-used tea set. I half expect her to suddenly vanish into one of the cups.

In the morning, I find her sitting on the veranda letting the sun warm her aging body. We share the house like the last surviving characters of a story: she has reached the final chapter, while I'm somewhere in the middle, trying to find my way to the end. She follows her daily routine without thinking twice, though she has her foibles just like everyone else, and she will not let sadness enter the house or sit down at the table.

We almost always speak Portuguese to each other rather than Crioulo, the Portuguese-based creole that is Cape Verde's common tongue. Like a reptile's skin, the old vernacular peeled off us long ago, but she says she still dreams of the house on São Nicolau, the roots of the tamarind tree that crept up the walls, the cool silence of its shade, the mule that was buried beside it. One day she asks me about the smooth stone slab we washed our feet on in the yard, then the conversation abruptly changes direction. Her manner of talking is like a spider leaping from one thing to the next. I'm left to wonder about how keen we all seem to be to reach the point where nostalgia feeds more off fantasy than memory.

She talks about that first night with him, when the clock on the wall struck midnight and she couldn't believe they'd been talking for two hours. The man who would become my stepfather took hold of her hands and her mouth felt bone-dry, as if she'd been out in the plains of Sal island rather than telling her brief life story. She wipes a speck from her eye as she remembers him saying the magic words: "I'll marry you and help you raise your children." My mother was always grateful for his good intentions, even if they couldn't last.

It was Christmas 1970. A few days after that conversation, they went to a Cape Verdean party together in Alcântara. They entered the bright, festive dance hall excitedly, arm in arm. I try to picture her happy and enjoying herself, perhaps even in love. She dances, laughs, bumps into old friends from the islands, and tricks her *saudades* into hiding away for the evening. The tables are laden with food and drink. Bana, the King of Morna, warms up the crowd before the band Luís Morais e Voz de Cabo Verde get the party jumping and a joyful homesickness grips the room.

My mother describes how quickly those young men, most of whom had immigrated to the Netherlands, forgot about the reality of their lives spent flitting between the glacial temperatures of the North Sea and the heat waves of the Persian Gulf. For the Christmas holidays, they sought shelter in the old metropole and the parties that reminded them of home. A few days later, they packed away their blazers, thin ties, and pointy shoes and made for Santa Apolónia train station. Before the week was out, they were sleeping on the North Sea waves again.

My mother breaks off into a tangent: the old water tank on São Nicolau. She talks about how it was surrounded by orange and banana trees, and remembers that we were always climbing on it or else sent on errands to fetch water from it with oil cans, cloths over our heads to protect us from the sun.

Somehow she drags me with her onto the playground of my childhood. Stories I'd forgotten elbow their way to the surface of my memory. My presence has awakened the past in my mum, offering blue skies or dark horizons, sometimes causing her to stare into the distance with a bittersweet expression on her face. Like many people, she clings to the secret hope that the islands haven't forgotten her, treasuring them as an idealized form of self-identity.

One day she takes a little longer than usual in the bathroom. I see her come out afterward, a white headscarf tied around her head and an old chamber pot in her right hand. She gives me a calm look that is at once defiant and distant. Her legs tremble under the weight of her body, and she stumbles a little before regaining her balance. I watch, concerned, from my bedroom door.

"It's fine," she says with a raised hand. But her eyes say more: *Yes, I'm old and worn out, and it might look to you like I'm going to die soon, but I won't, I can get by just fine on my own, how do you think I've managed all these years?*

She goes and sits down on the bed. I follow and look at her hands, bony and veined, her skin withered and hardened. Ridiculously, the idea strikes me that these can't be her hands. But they are, and I don't like to think of life running through those veins, so I look away.

She has what she calls "an upset tummy," a hereditary condition that afflicts all the women in our family. She'll be bedbound for the next twenty-four hours. How many more twenty-four hours has she got left? I try to banish the thought, even to interpret what I've just seen as life-affirming evidence that her legs are holding up well, that her arms remain strong, that her head is still marvelously functional, and woe betide anyone who says otherwise.

Without raising her eyes, she says, "I'm going to lie down and rest for a while, I'll call you if I need anything." She pulls up the cover and settles with the levity of a leaf falling to the earth.

I stand at the door for a moment before leaving. The Crioulo phrase *mi sô* comes to mind, its meaning something like "just me"; in other words, it expresses one's aloneness twice, but an aloneness that may well be wished for. Sometimes only the mother tongue can provide true refuge.

SIX

And out of nowhere two huge dogs appear and come charging toward me. Adrenaline floods my body, the ancestral fear of man against beast, predator turned prey. But though I can feel the blood pumping frantically through me, I remain rooted to the spot: there's nowhere to run to, and I've brought nothing to defend myself with. I'm done for.

Then a whistle pierces the air and the hounds come to an immediate halt. A shepherd emerges from the brambles down by the river, looking as surprised as me at this chance encounter. He utters a series of apologies as my heartbeat slowly starts to recover. I think about how unaccustomed he must be to finding strangers walking around here—as, evidently, must his two dogs. The cows that trail behind him, on the other hand, see me as only a mild curiosity. I walk through them and out the other side. The dogs carry on barking, desperate for a piece of me. Even when I'm a hundred yards away, they still stare at me, poised for their master to change his mind.

In many ways it's a bucolic image: the age-old allegiance between man and dog. I think about the 7,600-year-old skeleton found in Alcácer do Sal and about Homer's *Odyssey*. Twenty years after setting off for Troy, only Ulysses's wife, Penelope; his son, Telemachus; and his dog, Argos, believed in his return.

When Ulysses appeared in Ithaca disguised as a beggar, Argos recognized him instantly.

The peninsula at the mouth of the Sado is called Troy—Tróia in Portuguese—possibly in homage to the Greek myth.

I walk on, newly appreciative of the silence, until the chime of the Vale de Guiso church bell echoes down the river, the hum of it lingering in the air for a long time. The village sits on a hill, and as I walk toward it, I start to make out features: the church tower, white houses with red roofs. The whole cluster seems to hover above the trees and the fields, where piles of cut rice crops wait to be gathered in. White egrets speckle the landscape, scavenging. A herd of brown cows follows my progress with what seems to be a mixture of suspicion and admiration.

I hear the distant sound of a combine cutting then reversing, the same seesaw routine I'd watched earlier. Soon I'm walking alongside a rice field that's already been harvested. Clumps of stubble remain in the ground, each the size of a hand span, like bristles on a round wooden brush. I shuffle down an incline and try walking on the field. It's as soft as a mattress.

The valley becomes much wider as I approach the Herdade das Parchanas estate. The irrigation canal is raised on posts here, bending around the rice fields like an el train. The river itself chugs along, as docile as the cows grazing on its banks. On the far side, a farmer plows through a field in his tractor and responds only half in kind to my wave. The fields have yet to be harvested: again the impression is of being before a large yellow-green lake.

No wandering stranger would go unnoticed in these hills, and vast though the valley is, I sense the twitching of curtains. I come to a field that looks like a car park for farm machinery: combine harvesters, tractors, plows, deep-treaded tires, and all sorts of things I've never seen before, all of it lined up in neat rows on the ground.

The farmer I waved to earlier parks and gets out. He points to a building on the other side of the canal and a little bridge I can use to reach it. He greets me on the other side and invites me into a sort of function room. The brick walls display framed photographs of hunting parties, men dressed in camouflage with shotguns slung over their shoulders, hares and game birds hanging from their belts.

The man's name is Henrique, and he puts everything I've seen over the past two days into numbers. He says that one hectare of rice used to take ten people a full day to harvest; it's now done in an hour by one man and a machine.

Those machines cost 350,000 euros apiece, though he tells me his are all rented. They cut only right to left, which explains all the turning and reversing they're obliged to do. Henrique works forty-five hectares, which is roughly average for farmers in the region. Most are tenant farmers and survive on subsidies from the European Union, an average of 500 euros per hectare. I knew Portugal produced a fair amount of rice, but I'm surprised when he tells me that the Portuguese eat more rice per capita than almost any other population in Europe.

The cycle starts in March, when the soil is turned over with a tiller and the land is leveled, all according to computer-controlled parameters. After stray clumps of straw have been removed, the land is fertilized, then the canal sluice gates are opened and the fields are flooded. The water, which comes from the Vale do Gaio dam, is sold by the cubic meter: irrigating his forty-five hectares costs Henrique a cool 17,000 euros.

May is planting time, when seeds are sown using a tractor or a plane. The field will be dry again by the end of June, assuming that April and May aren't especially windy or hot, so weed killer and pesticide can be sprayed. The rice plants grow over the summer and are harvested in September and October. They should have some moisture in them when picked, then immediately be put to dry in one of the region's drying facilities.

Henrique says people used to come from all over Portugal for the rice season. Today machines do all the work.

Just as African slaves did when the industry began, I think.

It's not known exactly when rice cultivation started in Portugal, but it seems most likely to have been introduced by the Moors in the eighth to twelfth centuries. In the Sado valley, sporadic efforts at growing the crop became more substantial in the early eighteenth century, requiring a larger workforce. There were already some Black slaves laboring on farms, but it was hard to draw white workers or seasonal workers to the area because of its reputation for malarial fevers. This would appear to be the real reason Black slaves were brought in large numbers to the Sado valley, backed up by the convenient, pseudoscientific theory that African people, having come from a tropical climate, were more resistant to malaria.

Similar claims were made by the British in America, and there are further parallels with the history of rice cultivation in the antebellum South. Recent studies suggest that, besides forced labor, enslaved Africans brought technology transfer to the South Carolina rice fields based on knowledge gained growing rice on the West African coast for years, maybe even centuries.

There are two basic species of rice, with *Oryza sativa*, first domesticated in Asia, being the most common. Portuguese merchants traded for *Oryza sativa* in Indian Ocean ports and introduced the crop to the Upper Guinea coast of Africa in the sixteenth century. But *Oryza glaberrima*, the other, lesser-known species, had been domesticated in the Niger valley for a long time before that.

Like their South Carolina counterparts, some enslaved Africans put to work in the Sado rice fields would have had prior knowledge of and expertise in rice cultivation, particularly in mangrove waters heavy with salt. What innovations they might have introduced we'll likely never know, so scant are records from the time, but it seems fair to say they would have at least demonstrated honed skills and techniques.

I walk along a dirt road on the left bank of the river. I submit myself to both road and river, trusting that wherever they lead me will be inhabitable, maybe even hospitable. I get to thinking about life as a journey, a question of familiarity and distance, and about walking as a movement that precedes thought and leads to discoveries, of places but also ideas. So long as we learn as we go, which path we take and where we end up perhaps matter little.

The road is flanked by riverbank reeds on one side and cork, oak, and pine trees on the other. For a long time, it was the only road into São Romão and would have been used by anyone traveling to the village by car. Leopoldina's aunt, for example, who married a pharmacist in Alcácer do Sal.

For Leopoldina and the other children in the village, Aunt Francisca was the closest thing they had to a fairy godmother: a rich auntie who brought them cakes and candy from the big city. She was tall and well-built, with dark, velvety skin and a bold dress sense: big hats and bright-colored clothes. Leopoldina remembers her as being very sensitive toward nature and for painting watercolors, landscape pictures that captured the valley's summer torpor: houses at the foot of hills, storks' nests, the reeds around the river.

At Christmas, Francisca would bring fine fabrics for the women in the village and real coffee, which would replace chicory for as long as it lasted, filling the house with its fragrance. The coming of her car always heralded a brief respite from daily hardships. She never had children of her own, so had plenty of leisure time, and she enjoyed teaching Leopoldina and the other kids how to make honey and olive oil cakes, just as she'd been taught by an auntie when she was a child. She liked to spend long summer days down by the river, picking a secluded spot under the huge beech trees, then letting herself float in the cold water until her body turned pale.

The road would also have been used by Leopoldina's great-uncle Aurélio da Preta when he went to enlist in the Portuguese army. Leopoldina imagines him as being a happy-go-lucky lad then, rather than the troubled man she'd known. He returned from World War I with clear signs of trauma, though they were variously misunderstood or coldly dismissed by the family.

His behavior became increasingly erratic until he was finally diagnosed with manic-depressive tendencies, leading to several years spent in various institutions and asylums. Once, back in São Romão, he tried to strangle one of his nephews in the middle of the night. The family managed to stop him only by hitting him over the head with a shovel. He hanged himself in a hospital bathroom not long after.

The war service that had so damaged him was part of the East Africa campaign. His regiment was posted to northern Mozambique and charged with repelling German raids on Portugal's colonial territories. He fought in the Battle of Ngomano, in which German forces, desperate for supplies, staged a bloody last stand at the Rovuma (now Ruvuma) River. Curiously enough, this grisly experience made him the first member of the family to see Africa since his ancestors were snatched from it centuries earlier.

V

I used to look down Avenida Dom Carlos I from Dona Vi's balcony and marvel at the tunnel of lilac it became when the jacaranda trees were in bloom. I must've been about seven, while Dona Vi was a lady in her fifties. She had honey-colored eyes, copper-colored skin, and straight hair. I recall her fussing over the dusting of a framed photo of an old airplane that hung on the wall in the living room. She'd turned her apartment on the corner of Calçada da Estrela into a guesthouse for Cape Verdeans, and I remember us going there for tea and cakes once, after somebody's funeral. Dona Vi turned to my mother and said, "I don't have the strength for it anymore. They all come to my house to die."

She was quite a tough lady, but kind. She wheezed in the chest when she breathed and suffered from flatulence, letting out a little toot, followed by a "pardon me," whenever she struggled out of her chair. With time, she became thin, aged, and bitter, and she ended up bedridden with diabetes.

My mother and Dona Vi first met working in the laundry room at Sal Airport in the late 1950s. They served the Alitalia crews that made daily stopovers on Sal, cleaning and ironing their uniforms. They even learned a few words of Italian—*hei, stirare pantaloni mia*—and never tired of saying them whenever they met up. They always talked about the flight attendants, who were very nice to them and whom they would admire standing outside the hotel waiting for the jeep to take them into Santa Maria, the nearest town, or to the swimming pool at Espargos. It was said that these women even sometimes swam naked out by Palmeira, which became known as the Italian Beach, then sunbathed and drank martinis on the café terrace.

For Dona Vi, it all began one August morning in 1939, when an Italian ship entered the port of Pedra de Lume for the first time, bringing equipment and technicians. After scouting around, they chose a flat area where goats grazed on the outskirts of Espargos and began building an airport. Its initial purpose was as a layover for Linee Aeree Transcontinentali Italiane (LATI) planes that took mail back and forth between Italy and South America.

Over the next three months, the island's tiny population, no more than a thousand or so, watched as a ready-made town emerged: a runway with two metal hangars for planes, repair workshops, a radio control tower (capable of providing air assistance right along the West African coast and as far as Brazil), a weather station, warehouses, offices, an electricity station, a hospital, and a thirty-bed hotel complete with a colonial-style bar, restaurant, and ballroom. The problem of securing a regular supply of drinking water was solved by drilling wells and building a cistern, which even allowed for the irrigation of a vegetable patch, and was backed up by the storage of thousands of bottles of mineral water.

Vicência Brito, the woman I would later know as Dona Vi, had recently arrived on Sal from Boa Vista island. She was one of the first cleaners employed by LATI, and she soon met the company's director general, a young pilot and aviation ace named Bruno Mussolini, Il Duce's son.

Just before Christmas, the airport celebrated the arrival of its first flight, which brought fresh supplies and correspondence for the Italian staff. The plane was guided in by the radio control tower and used the flickering lights of neighboring Santiago as a visual reference point. When the weather allowed it, the pilots learned to orientate themselves on the approach to the archipelago by seeking out the cone of the volcano on Fogo.

In the 1930s, Italian civil aviation was among the most advanced in the world. Using trimotor planes, LATI became the first company to run a guaranteed transatlantic postal service. It ran weekly return flights on three routes: the European route, which went from Rome to Seville to Lisbon to Villa Cisneros to Sal, with a night's stopover on Sal (the route was "European" in that Cape Verde was considered Portuguese territory and Villa Cisneros [now Dakhla] in Western Sahara was under Spanish rule); the Atlantic route, from Sal to Pernambuco, in Brazil's northeast; and the American route, from Pernambuco to Rio de Janeiro.

In May 1940, Bruno Mussolini embarked on a tour of all the stops on LATI's postal route. Having completed his inspection of Sal, he was preparing for the onward leg to Brazil when he got a phone call telling him to fly back to Rome immediately: Italy had gone to war with France and Great Britain.

By the following month, flights on the postal run to Brazil had been reduced to one per month. Brazil declared war on Italy in December 1941, and with the United States also entering the fray, LATI canceled its transatlantic service. Peace and quiet returned to Sal. The Italian staff members stationed on the island were all repatriated.

All except one. Luigi Salvi, the site manager, stayed behind to watch over the equipment.

The older generation of Sal islanders remember him sitting on the terrace, desolate, staring into the distance. Vicência still went to the airport every day to clean his office. Salvi was tall, around forty years old, with sun-kissed skin and windswept hair. But Vicência barely looked at the man she invariably found sitting at his desk, writing in his notebook and smoking a pipe. Sometimes he fiddled with the radio, trying to get news of the situation in Europe. After reading any correspondence that might have come in on the boat from Lisbon, he would get in his jeep and go and chat with the fishermen at Pedra de Lume. Then one morning he asked Vicência if she'd like a cup of coffee, and so it began.

For a long time afterward, people would talk of seeing them out on picnics, drinking champagne as the sun set on a remote beach. One day he told her he was going to São Vicente to meet the crew of an Italian ship, the *Gerarchia*, which had been impounded by the Portuguese authorities at Porto Grande. Would she like to come? She'd never been to São Vicente carnival before, and together they roamed the streets and cafés of Mindelo, touring the dance halls until dawn. While Europe reeled in the storm of war, they danced the night away at the Café Royal.

One day news came in that the war was over. Luigi Salvi went into the warehouse and took out two bottles of Chianti. He put a record on the gramophone, and they celebrated listening to tarantellas.

In 1947, a vanquished Italy had its airport concession revoked. The Portuguese government made Italy a risible offer to buy the facilities, an offer it could not, of course, refuse. The alternative was to dismantle the base and ship everything back to Italy by sea at great cost. In January 1948, Salvi took a last look at the air base, bid Vicência farewell, and got on a boat bound for Italy.

The Italians started using Sal again in the 1950s as a refueling stop for Alitalia flights to Buenos Aires and Caracas. For a while, every time Vicência heard a plane come in, she rushed to the runway to see who'd landed. But it was never Salvi. By the time it was Sophia Loren, a few years later, Vicência was engaged to a Portuguese airport official and packing her bags to move to Lisbon.

SEVEN

And then at long last I see São Romão in the distance. The village where Leopoldina was born appears nestled at the foot of the hill like a nativity scene.

The road I've been following through the flats turns into a bridge and crosses the Sado. The water is much more substantial here, and there are water lilies growing in the riverbanks and lily flowers in the shadow of the bridge, each one the eye of a storm of insects. On the other side of the bridge is the village.

A bus stop, sad looking and abandoned, welcomes the visitor. Most of the houses are single story and painted white with blue or yellow borders, as they are in almost every village in the Alentejo. A little boy plays with a dog in a rudimentary children's playground. A sign on the wall next door, written in blue ink, says that the house is for sale along with some land below the church, 3,750 square meters in total. A dark-skinned woman comes out of the house on the other side and heads over to the child. They both stop and stare at me for a while.

Two plastic tables flank the door to the village café, their red color faded by the sun. Half a dozen matching chairs are stacked in a corner. A notice in the window says the café is closed. A woman opens a window to tell me it's not just closed for now; it has closed down.

At the end of the road, I see a public washhouse. I walk down and fill my water bottle from the tap. The space has a split-roof covering so that both sides of the trough are shaded. Across from me, on the other side of a crossroads-cum-town-square, two women are perched on a precarious form of metal scaffolding, whitewashing the wall of a house. Most of the houses are in ruins, while those that look inhabitable appear to be abandoned.

It's hard to picture this as the place Leopoldina described to me. She spoke of a village full of life, of strapping men working the fertile soil, of gossiping women watching over mischievous children, of frisky, hotheaded youths. There is no sign of this vital energy, no hint of man's dominion over the land or wholesome childhoods spent running through the marshes, wild and free. Quite the opposite, in fact. An unfiltered nothingness pervades the air, a futureless void with nothing on the horizon but death. São Romão has become a ghost town.

It takes me no more than a few minutes to walk around the two solitary streets, entwined in a sort of figure eight. I take a chair and sit down at one of the tables outside the closed-down café, eager to rest my bones after what has already been a ten-hour day.

I pluck out my notebook and bleakly hope that what I jot down might somehow add up to something significant to bring back to Leopoldina—that the gaps between my annotations might turn into bridges like the ones that connect the different sections of the mudflats. The only alternative is to embrace the desolation of the place and the futility of my venture, to accept that I've walked for days to reach the epitome of nowhere.

The village bears no resemblance to *a ilha de pretos* (the island of the niggers) that José Leite de Vasconcelos wrote about, employing what he claimed to be a popular term for the place among locals. The famous ethnographer first visited what was then called São Romão do Sádão in 1894—just twenty-five years after slavery was outlawed outright in Portugal—and reported his findings in the inaugural issue of *O arqueólogo português,* an archaeology magazine, in an article entitled "The Race of African Origin." Noting that the African influence in Portugal was twofold, based on ancient conquests of Portugal by African people and modern conquests of Africa by Portuguese people, and evident throughout Portugal, he went on to say that what he found in the Alcácer do Sal valley was different, "a colony, albeit circumscribed."

Clearly intrigued, he returned to the place and subject in 1920 for his *Boletim de etnografia,* a five-volume encyclopedia compiled for the National Museum of Archaeology, which Leite de Vasconcelos himself had founded. He included photographic evidence this time, an example of what he called "a Portuguese specimen of the Black race." The photo is of a man with dark skin and gray sideburns wearing a fisherman's cap. He has a pipe in his mouth and smiles for the camera.

Leite de Vasconcelos called the villagers *mulatos* but reported that they referred to themselves as *atravessadiços*—"crossbreeds." He said that their skin color varied—some were darker, some were paler, and some were quite black—but that the place could no longer properly be called "the island of the niggers," not because it was an offensive term but because of the whitening process that was under way.

As I sit outside the closed café, I try to imagine the look on Leite de Vasconcelos's face when he first came upon the people he described as dark-skinned, fuzzy-haired, and flat-nosed. He said that he'd heard tell you could still smell the savanna on some of them.

I see the woman from the playground again, carrying two buckets of water down the road. I get up, say hello, and introduce myself as a friend of Leopoldina. She puts her buckets down and looks at me, and I immediately sense the history in her: the color of her hair and skin, her swarthy complexion, the silence of her stare; it all speaks to me of São Romão do Sádão's storied past. I can clearly see in her the generations of Black people who were born, lived, worked, and died here.

Her name is Etelvina, she eventually says. She remembers Dona Leopoldina the primary school teacher very well, of course. She says that, like the teacher, almost everyone from back then has left the village; some went to Alcácer do Sal, others to Setúbal, others to Lisbon. There are only twelve inhabitants left in the village now.

She seems keen to get on with her business, but I tease out the conversation as best I can. The boy I'd seen playing is her grandson; Etelvina is a widow, the child's parents work in Setúbal, and she looks after the boy during the day. I want to ask her about the history of slavery in the village. Instead we talk about how there are no other children in the village for the boy to play with, but how he keeps her company and how the arrangement saves his parents from having to pay for a *crèche*, for God knows times are tough and the economy is hardly booming around here.

She sets off again, leaving me to ponder in my notebook on the disconnect between existence and history. We exchanged pleasantries, but establishing any kind of dialogue with her about the village's past seemed an impossibility. She answered me, the passing traveler, out of politeness and goodwill, but with little interest. I got no sense that she knew or would have liked to know about the old slaves. I wonder whether Leopoldina will remember her, what she might have to say about Etelvina. For despite her lack of engagement, the long intervals between my questions and her answers revealed a vague, undefined nostalgia. Her answers were contained, windows to an abyss, incongruities left hanging in the air.

Etelvina won't leave the village any time soon, I don't think, at least that's not what her eyes said as they cast downward, her gaze piercing the ground. There's the house to look after, the orchard at the back, her grandson. She's not an old lady yet, but she long ago ceased to be a Sado valley girl with bright black eyes and a fresh face. A gentle wind runs down the street like a phantom and ruffles her black dress. The image, her blithe sense of rugged resistance, strikes me as being some kind of epilogue to Black history in the village.

A dirt track leads up to the church behind the village on the hill. The building is painted white with blue borders at the base and around the windows, just like the houses. Four of the windows are long, vertical, and shuttered. A smaller window above the main door takes the form of a cross. The belfry is only a little taller than the building itself. Its door, like the main door, is locked. The three-foot weeds outside suggest the bell hasn't tolled for some time.

The cemetery lies behind an adjoining white wall with an iron gate, padlocked and chained. I peek through the rails in the gate and see not a single laid flower. The dead here are doubly forsaken, denied even the noise of the shovel and the cadence of prayer. It looks like a pretend cemetery. Paradoxically, the place is full of life, home to numerous birds, rabbits, mice, and frogs.

I had hoped to find names that harked back to the slave era, but I'm blocked by an iron gate. Never mind the color of their skin, the dead here have been definitively forgotten, abandoned to rest in the peace of a secret garden. A family of birds comes chirping out from a row of cedar trees, and the air is pungent with the smell of wildflowers and figs. I feel a surge of happiness at being alive, the sort of physical joy that proximity to nature brings, and the view—over the village and across the river, the sun shining, cattle grazing in the fields—more than compensates for any frustration I might feel at not being able to poke around among the tombstones.

Back in the village, I find an elderly lady hanging washing on a clothesline. She tells me her name is Efrigénia. She has earthy skin and the amber eyes of people from Fogo. But when, more determined this time, I ask her about the slave populations that once inhabited the village, she looks at me astonished. With the calm assurance of those who have no need to consult the history books, she tells me no, not here; her people have always been white. I'm left with no choice but to change the subject, to nod along to the trivial things she tells me about the hardships of country living and getting by on her own as a widow.

While she talks, the long bloodlines that have led to her appear before me: the imperious march of miscegenation that has taken hold among these forgotten people of the valley. I ask about her childhood, but Efrigénia wants to talk about social injustice and oppression, the winds of change that have brought agrarian reform to the region. She speaks with melancholy and a rarefied memory for someone in her eighties, but without regret or remorse. She points out the house where she was born, and where her parents were born, and a fair few brothers and sisters besides. It is now not much more than a pile of rubble overrun with brambles, but it has just enough structural integrity to contain her memories and preserve a large chunk of her long life.

I ask her if she remembers Leopoldina. "Who?" she says. "The teacher," I reply. She thinks about it for a moment and then says no, that she left the village when she was eighteen to work in a canning factory in Setúbal and was away for the next ten years. Then she married a lad from Alcácer do Sal, and when he died, she returned to the village to look after her parents, a widow in her forties. She's been here ever since.

Before hanging each item on the line, she shakes it with epic vigor, and this seems to reflect the way she's lived her life: a mixture of tough love, patience, and tolerance of boredom. She's the sort of person who no longer fears death or finds any reason to cry; the troubles of the world appear alien to her. Her stoicism wavers only when she tells me of a neighbor, a childhood friend, crippled by illness, who was taken, against her will, away from São Romão to die in a hospital in Lisbon.

VI

Displays of racism from mixed-race people can be silent and subtle, conscious and unconscious. We can also sometimes adopt chameleonic affectations. Much of this is well known, but while there is ample literature on the Black experience, very little has been written about being mixed race, intriguing though it clearly is. Essays on mixed-race thinking—our anxieties, our position in society, our sense of place—are rare. One would struggle to find a James Baldwin–like figure reflecting on mixed-raceness and the ambiguous nature of our condition, perhaps because it is, in many ways, more complex, or at least more difficult to define. To define is to classify, with all the potential risks and mistakes that entails. And, of course, mixed-raceness may, ultimately, be more of a cultural phenomenon than anything epidermal.

Those responsible for racial segregation, on the other hand, have had no qualms in creating classifications in order to define rules. There is no room for ambiguity when it comes to the cold, hard stare of the legislator, no place for legal vacuums or voids. With definitions came habits and customs, as well as laws, not to mention punishments for transgressors. For some mixed-race people, definition came as a relief, but it made others more contemplative, others more distant. Some risked their position in "racial purgatory" by raising a hand, or perhaps a finger, in support of Black people. But being mixed race has almost always involved some degree of denial, the first reflex of an identity crisis, in this case of one's negritude. It has meant having to constantly fight against the doubts of self-persecution and the awareness that your place in society is directly linked to your lighter skin tone, and even then, precisely where you place is on a sliding scale.

Because of our founding history—the Cape Verde islands were uninhabited until Portugal colonized them and made them a base for the Atlantic slave trade—almost all Cape Verdeans are mixed race. We were afforded a better education than our colonized counterparts in mainland Africa. This enabled us to infiltrate the colonial apparatus of the Portuguese administration, and we took advantage of this, playing our part in a system that dominated Black African peoples. For evidence of our disgrace, one need look no further than the last captains engaged in the business of trafficking people, holdouts against the advance of civilization.

As a teenager in Lisbon, I found that schoolmates would include me when they made racist jokes about Black people, showing me, indirectly, up to exactly what point I could "pass for white." Mixed-race consciousness has always been a search for shelter, and cozying up to the white race and white culture has often provided a comfort zone. This has, it should be said, sometimes been a matter of survival, but it has nevertheless meant failing to venture into lesser-known, more complicated terrain.

Different skin tones have always existed in our family. The subject was what one might call a nonissue. Nevertheless, I have never heard my mother describe someone as tall, Black, and handsome, the same way she might refer to someone as being *"alto, branco branco, d'odj azul"* (Crioulo for "tall, white-white, and blue-eyed"). Her father, Francisco "Nênê," was *branco d'odj claro* (white and bright-eyed), naturally. In other words, the emphasis has always been placed on degrees of whiteness, not blackness.

Cultural prejudices and preconceptions turned us islanders into pretend whites and apprentice colonialists in our dealings with people from continental Africa. This pitiful form of wishful thinking showed itself whenever a *capataz* from Cape Verde (within Portugal's colonial machine, the *capataz* was a "foreman" figure or "overseer") sat in for a white *chefe de posto* (local governor) or *administrador do concelho* (regional governor) while he enjoyed a nice, long vacation in the metropole (Lisbon). It reared its ugly head whenever we drank whiskey of an afternoon or played tennis with the colonizers and experienced a momentary dizziness: *This could almost be us.* The social condition of being nearly white allowed us to frequent society parties and dances, and giddy from our glimpse of the good life, we lost our moral compass and cultivated the habit of disparaging the natives, scorning those whose blood ran in our own veins.

Centuries of relative isolation as an island people had opened up a chasm between us and mainland "heathen folk" who were blacker than us and "behind us" when it came to "values, civilization, and progress," deepening our cultural aversion for and distancing from them. Our sailors lived alongside such men, sharing boats on voyages around the world, but never considered them equals, even when their complexions were identical. The expression *preta fina* (fine nigger woman), a favorite term of older generations, uses the adjective "fine" almost as a counterbalance, as if to rescue the poor woman from her unfortunate skin color, while at the same time emphasizing it or assigning it a particular quality within the panorama of negritude.

Every mixed-race person can expect to experience the same anguish as Joe Christmas at least once in his or her life. William Faulkner's character in *Light in August* is a man trapped by the obscure mysteries of his Black roots and the contradictory feelings they provoke. I also remember how much I was affected by the plight of Philip Roth's enigmatic college professor Coleman Silk in *The Human Stain*. A light-skinned African American, Silk marries a white woman and passes himself off as Jewish, seeking to thus erase the blemish of his ancestry.

My existential doubt centered around whether we were, in fact, *pretos*, as some of the kids in school claimed. Perhaps they'd noticed how many dark-skinned people came in and out of our building, or the darker tones of certain family members who picked me up from school. But the wickedness of children is really its own story.

I never knew for sure what category we belonged to. Most of the time, we seemed to identify more with Black people, especially when, for example, we saw the Black Mozambican bullfighter Ricardo Chibanga triumphing in Lisbon's Campo Pequeno bullring. Older family members referred to whites as *mandrongos*, a disparaging Crioulo term of unclear origin (possibly Angolan, and possibly to do with offal) that seems headed for extinction. All that said, the contrasting skin tones of my relatives wasn't very helpful. My great-aunt Tanha, for example, was very dark-skinned with white hair that she wore in plaits that came down to her chest, while my aunt Mana not only looked completely white, but she also wore a wig and sunglasses and laughed as loudly as any rich white woman did, the better to show off her perfect white teeth.

Back in the 1960s, two seafaring uncles of mine were refused entry to a nightclub in Jacksonville, Florida. They told the story of being utterly baffled by what was happening: they were well dressed, wearing suit and tie, just like all the Americans in the queue, and they'd partied in a similar establishment in Panama City only a week before. But the club was for whites only, the doorman explained.

Both men were dark-skinned, but tall and slim with delicate facial features and thin, bony fingers. They claimed their thick hair had given them away. They liked to wear big gold rings and silver chain necklaces, and whenever they docked in Lisbon, they paraded around downtown Baixa as if they owned the place.

In the early '80s, something happened that shook the makeshift identity I'd built to its foundations. A single-column news story written by an unnamed journalist appeared in the *O Jornal* newspaper under the headline "The Cannibal of Odivelas," and as a result fear and suspicion spread like wildfire through Portuguese families, producing what might be described as a moment of genuine social hysteria.

The story, published in March 1981, recounted the alarming and tragic tale of Carla Cristina, an eight-year-old girl from Lisbon, who'd been attacked and killed by a Cape Verdean man. As if that wasn't bad enough, he'd gone on to devour her innards.

The sorry episode occurred in Odivelas, a peripheral Lisbon neighborhood near to where we lived, after the girl, who was white, had gone out bright and early to buy bread and milk. She was attacked on her way home by Augusto Dias Martins, a thirty-year-old from Santiago, employed on a building site nearby. He first threatened her with a knife and demanded that she hand over her groceries, then he attacked her. The girl's father, Francisco Figueiredo, told the newspaper that by the time he and his wife arrived on the scene, the girl was dead and the Cape Verdean man was eating her: she was bleeding from one ear and had two gaping holes in her stomach. Undeterred by their presence, the man continued to feast on the girl's insides and took flight only when Senhor Figueiredo started to pelt him with stones. The man ran away carrying little Carla's liver in his hands, blood and guts spilling from his mouth. The newspaper explained that he'd likely killed and eaten her to satisfy his craving for human flesh.

Beside the news story was an ad for an insurance company with a picture of a mother holding a baby tight to her chest: "My baby has an extra friend, an assured friend . . . a shield . . . a guarantee in difficult times."

A few days later, rumors emerged that the Cape Verdean cannibal had escaped from jail in Beja, a town in the Alentejo, and had been seen roaming the countryside in the company of two brothers, a sort of flesh-eating horde. Panic gripped parents throughout the Alentejo, while families in Lisbon arranged for their children to be picked up early from school.

Meanwhile, two long articles in *O Jornal* considered the curious case from the angle that had most shocked people: the phenomenon of anthropophagy played out right there on the streets of the capital. To supposedly gain a better understanding of the subject, and potentially ward off a public lynching, the newspaper assembled the opinions of several academics and psychologists under the headline "Explaining the Inexplicable: Horror Comes to the Land of Gentle Ways." (The Salazar regime liked to refer to Portugal as "*o país dos brandos costumes*," "the land of gentle ways.")

Apparently King Peter I, better known as Dom Pedro, had once chomped on the hearts of the men he'd had executed for having slain his beloved Inês. This mad gesture, born of love, still stirred the emotions of plebeians today, but Augusto Dias Martins, a Black man from the Cape Verde islands, had gorged on a living girl.

The whole topic was broached with a mixture of fascination and repulsion; "gentle ways" soaked in blood. Even then, I never quite understood the reasons the newspaper gave for what had happened:

1) Madness as a response to the humiliations of being an immigrant as expressed by lashing out at the elderly and children, the host society's weakest and most vulnerable.

2) Volition to be white, loved, and pure, as manifested in the man's resolve to consume an innocent little girl and, in particular, her liver. This was not a random body part but the noblest organ of all, perhaps even more important than the heart: no doubt the Cape Verdean man believed the liver to be home to the soul, an individual's source of strength and character.

The image of the Black Cape Verdean man feasting on the entrails of a white girl sent shock waves through the country and wreaked havoc with my immigrant's conscience. The public's imagination ran wild with visions of evil armies of cannibalistic Black men. In turn, the police were called at the smallest sign of even vaguely suspicious behavior. Extra vigilance was set up on public transport as a witch hunt began that targeted Cape Verdean students, construction workers, and cleaning ladies.

For years, I was haunted by the image of Augusto Dias Martins, a vague image that no doubt equated to some kind of aggregate of all the men I knew from Santiago. Also by the photo of the girl's parents, standing desperately before the blood-soaked body of their child, an image that most readers would have seen as but the latest episode in a lifetime of humble suffering. The tragic incident awoke in me strong feelings of recrimination about misfortune and fate, and bewilderment that such an inexplicable episode could change people's lives in an instant. I struggled with the idea of the father, forever traumatized by his loss, and the madman, talking to himself in the corner of a room in a mental asylum. I imagined him dreaming of the cornfields in Santa Catarina, on the western coast of Santiago, perhaps admiring the tallest ears blowing in the wind, unaware of the symbolism or syndrome, the imperfections of human nature.

EIGHT

And from amid the silence and birdsong of the mudflats, I suddenly hear canned laughter. I've left São Romão far behind, and I'm on my way to Rio de Moinhos, where Leopoldina taught primary school. I'm hoping it will be a big enough village for me to find somewhere to stay for the night, but for now I'm in the middle of nowhere. The laughter cracks through the silence again, and I'm sure my ears are playing tricks on me, until I see a man sitting at a table under a tree. He's a curious sight, out here in the woods, and he cuts a figure of enigmatic solitude. The shadow of the tree draws a perfect circle around him.

As I get closer, I realize the irrigation canal passes just ten feet away from him. The ground around him is covered in leaves and fallen fruit from the quince tree above. Middle-aged, dark-skinned, and curly-haired, he's listening to a comedy sketch show on an old transistor radio placed before him on the table. The original tabletop hangs broken from the frame, split down the middle, but rather than remove it, he's simply placed a new one on top. He's possessed of a slothful dignity befitting the environment that surrounds him, and when he finally notices me, it does nothing to speed up his movements.

Without fully disengaging from what he's listening to, he tells me he's the canal guard. With a little prodding, I learn that his work consists of opening the sluice gates and regulating the flow of water that irrigates the rice fields, a task that strikes me as being of almost heroic importance—a guardian of the waters. I stand and watch the water drifting by. In a lot of ways, this man is humbly regulating the flow of life itself, which maybe explains why he seems to inhabit a different time frame from mine. He looks very content. He'll doubtless be in another part of the valley tomorrow, sitting in the shade with his transistor radio, regulating the flow of the water there and trusting, blissfully, in the eternal laws of the universe to do the rest.

The man casts the odd inquisitive glance my way, presumably finding my lingering presence strange. But he doesn't ask me what I'm doing there or show any real curiosity in what's detaining me.

I think about telling him anyway, sharing my lofty thoughts and explaining the nature of my mission. I imagine he'd find the whole enterprise pointless and have no interest in the history of the region, but I'm merely speculating, filling in the gaps of his silence. Regardless, I sense something meaningful about the moment, some kind of broader truth that has perhaps been forgotten. The sun filters through the leaves of the tree and reflects off the surface of the water. But there's more to it than that. Despite the artificial nature of its banks, the canal performs the noble task of bringing life to the plains, and in this it serves an economic purpose in a way that the ancient river no longer does. Of course, the river is delivering water to the ocean, and though the two channels have different destinations and destinies, both are vital in their own way, and both provide nourishment to millions of microscopic creatures in their depths. It's just that in recent decades the worth of the canal has superseded that of the Sado, which is now prized primarily as a fun fact: it's the only major river in Portugal that runs from south to north.

I leave the man to his happy seclusion and set off again. In the sky above, the wind pushes little clouds along, dropping sudden islands of shade onto the sun-drenched landscape and sending fractured sunbeams into the dankest corners of the hillside.

I'm sometimes taken by a strong urge to be a part of this natural balance, to breathe it in, to sit down beside the canal guard and his radio, for instance, and simply belong without questioning. Perhaps what I aspire to is to be a little more than what I am, or what I think I am, how I see myself, as I walk through the beautiful green of the trees leaving footsteps that will soon be washed away by the elements. I catch a glimpse of my shadow, my small and insignificant silhouette, and can't help but think about the great river guardian's ancestors, most probably African slaves, and the journeys they made.

Back beside the river, I feel alone or somehow orphaned. I walk against the flow, toward the source, though I'm not seeking it; rather, I've gone in search of signs of life: tired looks, lost hopes, dreams reborn in the fresh grass. Here the Sado is hardly a river worthy of superlatives, but its unsteady flow and uncertain color are enough to inspire in me wistful thoughts about identity, delusions of grandeur, and the human condition. The river gains in vigor when it, like the irrigation canal, is buoyed by water from the Vale do Gaio dam. I watch leaves, sticks, and flower petals float serenely by.

The village of Rio de Moinhos comes into view through a gap in the trees. On the opposite slope I can make out the local primary school, where Leopoldina once worked, built in the "soft" style of the Estado Novo, an ornamental architecture favored by the Salazar regime. The closer I get, the more it looks like some kind of temple or church, but seeing it from afar also brings home the importance of education and the role that attaining literacy played in the social advancement of the children, grandchildren, and great-grandchildren of Black slaves in the region.

The way I'd sought to see what I wanted to see in São Romão suddenly seems silly. I'd tried to step back in time when what I should have been doing was embracing the facts, scattered by the wind and soaked into the soil though they may be. When we look to the past, hopes and fears, births and deaths, appear as if suspended from a single point on the horizon, but this is to ignore the great leap of human imagination that is time itself. Rather than turning back the clock, should I not be looking for the ways in which servitude has been shed from or projected into the spirit of the present?

With the sky turning red in the afternoon sun, I rouse myself for the final push to Rio de Moinhos, still some three miles away. As I pass through a series of gates demarcating hunting land, I think about different degrees of freedom. Looking at the river, I wonder whether I would be able to go with freedom's flow if parts of me were still protruding from the water. Freedom did not come rushing out after the sluice gates of captivity were opened; it was more of a drip, then a dribble. But did the first free generation feel the current behind them more than the eddies that held them back? When they took the plunge, what occupied their thoughts? What didn't?

I walk in between the hill and the river and imagine I'm walking a boundary between two worlds, the past and the present. But every footstep brings new doubts, and I find myself veering off toward the side of history. I wonder about Pedro Fogueiro and Aurélio da Preta, Leopoldina's great-uncles. What did they think about the circumstances of their ancestors? Or did they not think about them? How did they deal with the stigma of their skin color?

I sense that their generation, the neophytes of freedom, chose to draw a veil over history, perhaps overlooking the debt they owed to their forebears for securing such freedoms. Many embraced Christ, finding in his martyrdom a vital force and welcoming him into their humble homes, built on these very riverbanks, drinking him in as a thirsty traveler would a glass of water in the desert.

From what Leopoldina told me of their talk and customs, any connection her family might have had to the oceans, mountains, and forests of Africa had long ceased to be real. The ancestral continent had been wiped from their memories. Thoughts of Africa required too much of a leap of faith when everything around them had to be reconstructed—language, habits, bodies, and land—in a transition in which their own survival was at stake. How might we acquire a new identity, departing from servitude, without betraying our ancestry? What kind of harmony can follow on from fetters and collars? Can the Sado valley's rivers and forests replace a whole cache of memories and help forge a new spirit?

Must a new soul take flight like a butterfly and leave the world of its predecessors behind in order to properly embrace modernity?

So a veil was drawn over obstacles that lay in the path toward a new and individual legitimacy. But the new world needed a new map. To understand how slavery was swallowed by these men and women, we have to consider the way fatalism took root and how Christianity and Jesus dying on the cross got mixed up in all of it. Eventually, of course, the church had to address an entirely free congregation, and it did so by denouncing the ignobility of slavery and spouting homilies about innocent souls and the importance of a simple life of good intentions.

Here I am reminded of Dona Maria I, queen of Portugal from 1777, known as Maria the Pious. In Lisbon she kept seven Black dwarfs as slaves, a supposed show of tolerance and charity that was more an exercise in objectification and prejudice. A famous painting, *Mascarada nupcial* (*Nuptial Masquerade*), by José Conrado Roza, depicts the dwarfs in a mock wedding ceremony. This was most likely a routine they were obliged to perform for the royal court's amusement, for to add insult to injury, they were employed as jesters.

I was always most taken by Siriaco, his skin patched white from vitiligo. He alone stands nude in the painting, dressed in nothing but his own illness. Although the others are attired for comic effect, their clothing and shoes afford them a certain air of Christian visibility. They led short lives, and I often wonder who among them lasted the longest—Siriaco, perhaps, with his spectral aura—and about their internal rivalries and disputes. The bride in the painting, wearing an expression of intense sacred seriousness, is Dona Rosa, or Rosa of the Sacred Heart of Jesus, as she was baptized, the queen's favorite. She was from Angola, as was her groom, while the two musicians were from Mozambique. The others were all from Brazil, including an eighth dwarf, a

Tapuia Indian, who in the picture plays the role of cupid. All were wrenched from their homes to be placed in the pious queen's cabinet of curiosities.

I cross marshland again in my approach to the village, and some sort of conclusion begins to form in my mind. The reality of enslavement here was not quite one of chains, shackles, and whips. The Afro-Portuguese slaves of the Sado valley might be better thought of as serfs or, in some cases, dependent caretakers, Black men who lived in a hut on the estate and followed their white masters around performing maintenance tasks or helping to protect the property when, for example, the river burst its banks. Servile and reverential men obliged to lead compromised lives— showing not the least sign of revolt, for example—but who, in exchange for providing a sort of canine loyalty to their masters, were afforded certain comforts.

We tend to look at history like an oncoming train, each carriage rammed full of the events of past decades, whole centuries even, rushing by for us to contemplate, absurdly and ambiguously, from our contemporary vantage point. In other words, rather than traveling back toward it, we want the past to come to us, often so we can dominate it by fetishizing our particular passions. If slaves and masters, property and chattel, all traveled in the same train, they did not know they were on any kind of journey, much less where they were going to. And yet I'm searching for the tracks, unable to resist placing them on the horizontal plain of my contemporary reading.

Relics serve the same purpose to me, whether they're an amphora used at the Chafariz d'El Rei or a bucket at the São Romão washhouse. Yet if I'm looking for signs, it's because I can see that these people triumphed over human ignorance and social injustice. They defeated institutionalized evil through the simple decency with which they lived their daily lives. They may have chosen not to register their misfortune or record the predicaments that plagued their conscience, the utter wretchedness of being public or private property. But their spirit of moral rectitude and nonconformity lives on, I would say, in the eyes of their descendants. Past offenses have not so much been buried and forgotten as swept aside in defiance, in a refusal to dwell on and therefore legitimize a world that consumed itself.

We live in a time of great knowledge, in which scholars have written theses about almost every corner of the past. I feel more like a callow poet, an untried laureate appointed in the absence of anyone else and compelled to compose a few verses about the twelve remaining souls of a sleepy village, the last of the Sado Mohicans. For inspiration, I have Etelvina, Efrigénia, and the canal guard, their refusal to indulge me, their unyielding gaze, their stubborn sense of survival and fortitude.

The sun is already setting as I reach Rio de Moinhos. The walls of the bar-restaurant Café Alentejano are covered in bas-relief wood carvings of rural scenes, the iconography of almost every bar in the Alentejo: shepherds dressed in black overcoats and felt hats, farmhands bent double harvesting a field of hay, hillsides dotted with rows of houses under an orange sky. I put my rucksack down, sink into a chair, and order a cold beer. After flicking through a couple of newspapers lying on the table, I begin my now daily routine of putting my notes in order.

The dining room is accessible through a door by the bar. I ask the owners, a young couple, if I can see the menu and if they know of anyone with a room to rent for a night or two. The man makes a few phone calls, and the woman tells me there's lamb stew left over from lunch. I inevitably get that feeling of being the stranger who's washed up in some Wild West town after crossing the desert on his horse. But there's no pianola here, nor tables of men playing poker, just a TV pumping out a Portuguese soap opera and a few local men sitting alone with their beers.

I move to the dining room. When I've finished eating, Augusto, the owner, comes over to tell me there's a lady with a room for me to see. We walk through the silent village as night quickly falls. It's a single-story house with a front wall and an iron gate that opens onto the main street. I take the smallest room and am told I can use the bathroom, living room, and kitchen whenever I like.

After a long, hot shower, I sprawl out on the bed. The room is simple. There's an enormous old gray TV that doesn't seem to work, an empty bookshelf, a table with two chairs, the bed, and a bedside table. A narrow window above the bed looks onto the street, and there's a light on the bedside table in the form of a globe. When I switch it on, the continents light up, individual countries glowing red or green, the oceans a yellow brown. A scroll in the Pacific Ocean proclaims the Historic Illuminated Globe:

© 1980 SCAN-GLOBE A/S
Denmark
Cartography by: Karl-F. Harig
Print by: E. Gieseking

My eyes fall upon a sketch of James Cook (1728–1779) off the coast of New Zealand, and I follow the line that traces his journey through the Pacific Ocean, until I reach the Tuamotu Archipelago and find Fernão de Magalhães, or Ferdinand Magellan (1480–1521), as he's called here, his name after abandoning Portugal for Spain. He's looking pleased with himself for having just navigated his eponymous strait. I spin the globe a little to the right and am surprised to see Bocage, Setúbal's great poet, lurking off the Mexican seaboard, until a caption informs me it is Alexander von Humboldt (1769–1859), the German naturalist who descended the Orinoco. Farther east, Christopher Columbus (1451–1506) emerges, hat on head, adrift in the wide Sargasso Sea.

Given the globe's date, it's perhaps only natural that the trajectory of the Skylab satellite is marked, launched May 14, 1973, from the Kennedy Space Center in Florida and falling back to Earth in Australia on July 11, 1979. We also have the Soviet Union, Yugoslavia, North Yemen and South Yemen, and Ethiopia bordering the Red Sea with no sign of Eritrea. I see Vasco da Gama

(1469–1524) approaching India in the Arabian Sea and trace his journey back around the Cape of Good Hope, where I meet James Cook again, now in the South Atlantic Ocean, halfway between Angola and Brazil.

The CAPE VERDE ISLANDS has Santo Antão, São Vicente, São Nicolau, Fogo, Sal, Boa Vista, and São Tiago islands marked, along with Mindelo and Praia. Underneath them is a drawing of a galleon with dates to the left and right: 1497–1498 for Vasco da Gama's voyage to India and 1519–1522 for Magalhães's first circumnavigation of the globe, both journeys having stopped off at Cape Verde. Continuing north, I reach PORTUGAL, with Porto and Lisbon labeled, the latter underlined.

VII

Before writing about the search for the great white whale, Herman Melville sailed the world's oceans in the company of many a Cape Verdean shipmate. In a short story entitled "The 'Gees" (an abbreviation of "Portuguese"), Melville refers to Cape Verdean sailors, specifically men from Fogo island, as being Portuguese. In what is doubtless one of the first examples of Cape Verdean people appearing in any American publication, Melville has his narrator recount, and indeed display, all the prejudice and disdain American sailors felt for these singular men, whom they considered inferior to them. The narrator also mentions the ash expelled from the volcano on Fogo and the island's great poverty, describing fish as the one and only food resource.

"The 'Gees" is a satire, and at first reading it is not entirely clear why Melville turned his attention on the Cape Verdeans—out of sympathy, solidarity, and compassion, or contempt for them as sailors?

Melville's narrator, an old sea dog, describes Cape Verdeans as being small of stature but brave, with a great capacity for work when the moment suits them. They are said to lack imagination but to have great appetites, to have huge eyeballs but little insight, to possess mouths that are too big for their bellies. They have short necks and round, compact heads, which the narrator takes to be a sign of solid understanding. Their teeth are strong, durable, square, and yellow, and their bodies have a peculiar odor—like the Negro, but not quite the same.

It is intriguing, and somewhat bewildering, that Melville's narrator does not consider the Cape Verdeans to be Black. Their hybrid complexion, he says, puts them in a sort of limbo that allows for all kinds of classification. In speaking of the islands, there is an indulgent tone to his stating that "all the likelier sort were drafted off as food for powder, and the ancestors of the since-called 'Gees were left as the *caput mortum*, or melancholy remainder."

Cape Verdeans became known to American skippers in the early nineteenth century, when whaling ships docked at Fogo seeking crew hands. By the time Melville wrote his story, in 1856, men from Fogo were to be found on almost every American whaling ship.

The reason is less prosaic than might at first be imagined. In Melville's story, Cape Verdeans are favored because they demand no wage whatsoever, working in exchange only for biscuits, which are dished out almost as liberally as the cuffs and blows the men receive. But many captains also judged the 'Gees to be physically and mentally superior to American sailors, who were liable to cause trouble if conditions were not to their liking.

Be that as it may, Melville's narrator points out that it is unwise to sail with a crew comprised entirely of Cape Verdeans because of their clumsy feet. Inexperienced Cape Verdeans—"green 'Gees"— were liable to fall off the rig and into the sea on the first stormy night.

But they were always ready to sail, he says, just as long as you waved a handful of biscuits at them, so the important thing was to be a good judge of them, which meant you had to study them as you would a horse: "simple as for the most part are both horse and 'Gee, in neither case can knowledge of the creature come by intuition." A captain was therefore advised to stand three paces in front of a potential recruit and look him up and down to gauge his stature and to take in the shape of his head, the size of his ears, the state of his joints, his legs, and his chest. It was wise not to hire a Cape Verdean on a fellow countryman's recommendation, for a captain from New Bedford had taken a man on board who, at the first gathering in of the sail, had hitched up his trousers to reveal shins plagued by elephantiasis. On a long sperm whaling voyage, the captain had been unable to disembark the man and ended up sailing him and his elephantiasis around the world for three whole years.

Melville's satirical text mocks ignorance in general, but in particular targets the scientific community and the racist research masquerading as ethnology that was highly prevalent in the United States and Europe at that time.

It was no less true, however, that Cape Verdeans in the United States—be they white-skinned, mixed race, or Black—went to great pains to distinguish themselves from Black Americans. All Cape Verdeans, a mixed-race island people, feared being "mistaken" for ordinary Black people, and such complexes and contradictions hold true today, wherever Cape Verdeans are and no matter how much they try to hide it.

The daughters of Cape Verdean immigrants in New Bedford often refused to socialize with their Afro-American neighbors and were always at pains to remind people of their origins as Portuguese citizens. They were living out to the letter what James Baldwin would later call "the price of the ticket," a bargain made by everyone who entered America: the price to "become white."

"I am not a colored man. I am from the white race. I was born in Portugal." So said Sweet Daddy Grace—Marcelino Manuel da Graça, to give his real name—born on the island of Brava, who categorically refused to be considered an African American.

"These papers call me a 'Negro.' I am not a Negro, and no Negro in this country can do what I am doing."

However, the church that Grace founded in 1919 in Massachusetts, the United House of Prayer for All People, prospered primarily off the faith of African Americans, the very people Bishop Grace refused to identify with. At a trial hearing in 1934—Grace was regularly accused of tax evasion—when asked if he considered himself to be of the Black race, Grace replied, "I do not consider myself anything but human."

Indeed, as a rule, evangelical pastors have always preferred to avoid the race question. Unlike my uncles in Jacksonville, Grace claimed never to have been subjected to Jim Crow segregation laws on account of his skin color and said he was loved by whites and Blacks alike. Grace was born in Cape Verde, but like my grandfather Francisco "Nênê," he considered himself Portuguese. He was convinced that he belonged to the white race, perhaps in order to continue to reason according to the racial categorizing he grew up with on Brava.

With his dark complexion, shoulder-length hair, beard combed through with cornflower, blue velvet cape, and two-inch fingernails painted green, red, and blue, Grace was nothing if not a flamboyant figure. His public tirades were outrageous: "If Moses came here now, he would have to follow this man," he said, pointing at his own chest. Or: "If you sin against God, Grace can save you, but if you sin against Grace, God cannot save you."

My knowledge of Grace's extraordinary life is mixed up with the life of my great-uncle David. It was my mother, in particular, who delighted in reeling out tales of our immigrant relatives, especially at family reunions. The American adventures of Grandad Nênê and his brother David always stirred my imagination, as did a photo we had of my grandfather taken on São Vicente in 1918: a young man with short hair, bright eyes, and tight lips. In 1907, age seventeen, he'd boarded a three-master as a cabin boy. Sometime later, he and his brother showed up, suitcases in hand, at my aunt Maria Cardoso's house in New Bedford.

Nênê worked as a welder, a machine operator, and, ultimately, a harpoonist on whaling boats in New England. David was more the free spirit, a man of many dubious occupations. He seems to have made a living from gambling, either by betting himself or by running numbers games and books on horse racing or boxing throughout Massachusetts, Rhode Island, and Connecticut. It was also said, around the docks at New Bedford and Nantucket and in the bars of Fox Point, Providence, that he'd gotten involved with a gang of Portuguese smugglers operating out of Provincetown, led by Captain Manuel "Manny" Zora. At night, David and Nênê and Jack Barreto, a friend from São Nicolau, trained as boxers at an Italian gym above a garage on Acushnet Avenue. David became the king of bar brawls and spent many a cold night in the New Bedford police cells waiting for Nênê or Jack to come bail him out. He later went to California. He didn't make his fortune there, but he became a sort of wise guy, a man of means, no questions asked.

Nênê was more sensible. He loved São Nicolau and went back every two years, his visits often resulting in the birth of a child. When his brood numbered three, he began to make improvements on a house he owned on the island, whitewashing it and buying up land around Cabeçalinho and Morro Braz, keeping some of it dry and irrigating the rest. He'd leave New Bedford harbor with beds and tables in the hold, mahogany chairs and the finest cabinets. In the late 1920s, he brought the first gramophone to São Nicolau, which became a fixture in the lounge alongside photos of the *Titanic* and the *Lusitania*. My mother said that on one of his Atlantic crossings, when he was returning to Cape Verde to get married, he heard something bashing against the hull of the *Ernestina*. A piece of wood had broken off, and there was a serious risk of it damaging the rudder and leaving the ship stranded. Nênê had twelve boxes of furniture and crockery in the hold, and when he saw that none of the crew was prepared to go and see what the problem was, he took off his shirt, tied a rope around his waist, and jumped into the sea. He fixed the problem in no time, but when he got home to São Nicolau he cried like a little boy.

Nênê used to ride a horse down from Pombas to the town of Ribeira Brava. In the rainy season, he'd put on rubber boots and a black oilskin coat and head out into the rain, smiling away, much to the bemusement of his wife and children. One afternoon, at the age of forty-nine, he fell off his horse and died. David wasted no time in making off with all his money, forging the paperwork and presenting himself at the bank as his brother's sole inheritor.

David was large, with small hands and chubby fingers. My mother remembers him traveling up the Caleijão road on a mule, dressed in a wide-brimmed hat and shiny gaiters. Uncle Dav, as she still calls him, first met Marcelino when he and the future Daddy Grace worked as cranberry pickers on Cape Cod. Marcelino married a girl named Jennie, from a Brava island family called the Lombas, and David would call by their house on South Water Street with sweets for the couple's kids, Irene and Norman. But David hadn't heard from Marcelino for several years when, walking through the center of New Bedford one day, he noticed an assembly of people in a room across the road. The people were all Black, and it appeared to be a sort of communion, but in the form of a party, complete with a live band. There was a man standing at the back, addressing the room, and people were listening to him intently. His voice sounded familiar. David approached and saw that it was none other than Marcelino, who welcomed David with a big smile.

Marcelino Manuel da Graça had made way for Charles M. Grace, a metamorphosis that had seen him abandon Jennie and their children to answer "the call of God" sometime around 1919. He toured across the United States, preaching and setting up places of worship wherever he sensed traction, building his first House of Prayer in West Wareham, Massachusetts. Another soon followed in New Bedford, on Kempton Street, which is where my great-uncle David came across him that night.

As the Houses of Prayer attracted increasing numbers of worshippers, so "God's intermediary on Earth" needed more help from collaborators, meaning a new line of work for David. Around this time, the Great Migration saw millions of African Americans leave the South and settle in cities in the North: Chicago, Cincinnati, Washington, Baltimore, New York, Minneapolis—places that needed workers and where there was more racial tolerance. It was these Black workers, most of them illiterate, who lapped up the message of hope delivered by Grace and other Black religious leaders, including Father Divine.

Unlike the eccentric Daddy Grace, photos from the period show Father Divine to be a man of sober appearance. Short in stature, with a bull-like neck and a bald head, he wore well-cut suits with a waistcoat, a stripy tie, and a handkerchief tucked in the breast pocket. Father Divine spent most of his time fraternizing with the faithful and at fundraising dinners and lunches. He found it hard to contain his strident voice and was forever prone to belting out apotheotic gospels. Black neighborhoods like Harlem were his fiefdom, and the arrival on the scene of new pastors like Charles Grace could only have been seen as a threat.

Grace performed a series of "miracle" acts of faith healing in Savannah, Georgia, in 1926, significantly boosting the numbers of his followers. Uncle David and his fellow assistants had their work cut out arranging mass meetings in tents and organizing gatherings that became genuine public events. Collective "baptisms" typically took place in swimming pools built beside the Houses of Prayer or else in nearby lakes and rivers that Grace "blessed" beforehand. In cities, Grace often resorted to "the divine shower": baptisms using curbside fire hydrants. One photo from the time shows him waist-deep in water in a swimming pool in Augusta, Georgia, with a crowd of worshippers gathered around him; Grace is dressed in black and the six followers, dressed all in white, wait to be baptized. It was around this time that some people began calling him the "Black Christ."

An incident in Seversville, North Carolina, almost ruined Grace's career forever. During a collective baptism in a river, one of his flock slipped and was dragged out by the current. Grace swam after him and tried to bring him back to land, but the panic-stricken man kept thrashing around. After several failed attempts to rescue him, Grace swam back to the riverbank, exhausted. The man drowned, and Grace returned to his task, baptizing the rest of the crowd.

"I think it was good for the man," he would say later. "It was a beautiful way to die, don't you think so? He was working for the glory of heaven and he must have had a beautiful death."

By then, Grace had taken to sitting atop the "Holy Mountain," a stagelike platform with several levels, at the peak of which was a throne. From there he proffered his words of wisdom, sometimes using Portuguese and sometimes Crioulo, to a background of trombone music and the ecstatic cries of his most fervent followers. Grace claimed that talking in foreign languages, or "speaking in toungues," as he called it, was a sign of true communion with God. "God does not answer your prayers when you use your own language. God wants us to speak his language, not your language."

My great-uncle David would have had a front-row seat as his old pal from the fruit fields began to believe his own myth and turned into the persona he'd created, a man predestined to fulfill a particular role in history. According to my mother, Uncle Dav was not so much one of Grace's "auxiliaries," as fundraisers were known, as one of his men on the ground. He was part of the team that took care of preparations ahead of Daddy Grace's arrival in a particular place—"Daddy Grace is in town, come one and all, and listen to the man of God!" The team booked the brass bands that would announce his arrival and a Cadillac or luxury Packard for him to parade around in, waving to the crowds. It also handled merchandise, items that Grace had "blessed": handkerchiefs bearing Grace's image, copies of *Grace Magazine*, Grace toothpaste, Daddy Grace Allwater Soap. "People can even be cured by touching a piece of paper I throw away," said God's intermediary on Earth. Or indeed, "Never mind about God. Salvation is by Grace only . . . Grace has given God a vacation."

By the late 1930s, Harlem was home to the largest Black community in the United States. Perhaps inevitably, it became the setting for the showdown between Daddy Grace and Father Divine. Besides the Harlem of the theaters, jazz, and the renaissance, there was also the Harlem of violence and poverty, with jobs ruined and families destroyed by the 1929 crash. Father Divine moved his International Peace Mission there in 1932, establishing a number of centers, called "Heavens," including his headquarters, Heaven No. 1.

According to newspaper articles from the time, Grace, having supposedly taken offense at Divine declaring himself to be God, inquired into the real estate status of Divine's headquarters. It just so happened that the bank that leased the property to the International Peace Mission was open to selling it. Without further ado, Grace paid the $2,000 deposit and arranged to buy the building. With a hall able to seat five hundred people, it would make an ideal House of Prayer.

It was an audacious stunt, and the press delighted in talking up the power struggle between the two Black religious leaders. After completing the purchase, Daddy Grace summoned journalists to the four-story building on West 115th Street to tell them he'd decided to kick the self-proclaimed God out in order to install his own House of Prayer headquarters there. "I will not drive him out of Harlem," Grace said of Father Divine. "I will just let him stay. Poor fellow . . . I will give him peace and pity." The "holy war" amused the press no end, and with the deal done and Grace poised to fly to Cuba, the newspapers printed his parting shot: "Go explain to your flock how come God Almighty can be evicted!"

By buying Heaven No. 1, Grace learned something that pleased him no end: another way to acquire power was by purchasing real estate. Over the next few years, Grace bought no fewer than forty-one properties, using donations from followers that he then "administered." Purchases included the Savoy Theatre in Newark, the Oriole Theatre in Detroit, and the El Dorado apartment building in Manhattan, as well as houses for him to live in that grew steadily larger: a twenty-room pile in Newark, a fifty-four-room villa in Detroit, an eighty-five-room mansion in Berkeley Square, Los Angeles. Grace already owned property in Los Angeles, including a converted hotel on West Adams Boulevard that still bears his name today, the Grace Apartment Hotel.

Farther afield, Grace acquired a ranch in Brazil and a holiday home in Cuba. Uncle David never got to visit those, but he saw most of the other properties and became well acquainted with the East Coast of the United States, accompanying Grace on annual July, August, and September tours through Buffalo, New Haven, New York, Philadelphia, Wilmington, Baltimore, D.C., Newport News, Norfolk, Winston-Salem, Charlotte, Columbia, Augusta, Savannah, and Miami.

In the early 1930s, a skinny young House of Prayer devotee named Minnie Lee Campbell almost destroyed Bishop Grace's reputation when she accused him of attempted rape. At trial, she said the incident had occurred after he'd given her a lift to Philadelphia and that several days of sexual harassment had followed, once she'd agreed to work as his cleaner. She later recounted, in a trembling voice, that she had previously had sexual relations with him in exchange for a job as a pianist at the House of Prayer in Baltimore—apparently Grace was very fond of hearing the psalms played. A child was born from this questionable relationship, but Grace refused to recognize it. John Hero, his private chauffeur, testified to the innocence of his boss, and the House of Prayer made sure that the transcript of his court declaration reached reporters. "It is all untrue," said Hero, "Daddy Grace is pure."

Family relations were certainly not Grace's strong point. He fell out with Irene, and Norman died young. While his son's funeral took place in New Bedford, Grace, unperturbed, continued with his evangelizing work in Charlotte. He did keep in touch with Marcelino, the product of a second marriage to Angelina, a woman of Mexican descent. Marcelino ended up in a psychiatric ward suffering from schizophrenia, before escaping and disappearing for over a decade.

Grace seems to have gotten along better with members of his House of Prayer family. These included Manuel Rose, whose son, Mário "Marty" Rose, made a film of his trip to Cape Verde in 1937. The forty-four-minute film was shown to raise money for the Seamen's Memorial Scholarship Fund in New Bedford, and Grace arranged a screening in his own living room. It was likely the first time images of Cape Verde had been seen on the big screen.

The film begins with footage of the bay at Porto Grande, on São Vicente, before moving on to the old Rua do Telégrafo and then taking in a PE lesson at the Liceu Gil Eanes. We then journey to São Nicolau, where Marty captured a religious procession going up Monte Sentinha. The images show worshippers following a priest up the hillside beneath a burning sun. On Brava, Marty filmed the Bay of Furna and a wedding procession, the bride and groom riding to church on a horse led by musicians through the streets of Nova Sintra.

After this visit to his parents' homeland, Marty returned to the United States and went into training to become a spy. The film, his background, and the geostrategic importance of Cape Verde saw him recruited by the Office of Strategic Services (the precursor to the CIA) with a view to his being placed on the islands. He moved to New York to study codes and other forms of secret correspondence. When America entered World War II in 1941, Marty enlisted in the U.S. Air Force. On his first day, officers asked all the Black recruits to step to one side. Racial segregation extended through all branches of the armed forces, but Marty decided that if the officers themselves couldn't distinguish between whites and Blacks, he wasn't going to do it for them.

He was sent to Florida, where he trained to be a B-17 gunner. His unit, the Eighth Battalion, was dispatched to England, and from an air base there he made regular bombing raids on France and Germany. Eventually a German fighter jet, its pilot having been shot, crashed into his B-17. Marty managed to bail out and pull the cord on his parachute just before passing out. He would later say that all he remembered of the incident was waking up in a field surrounded by German country folk armed with pitchforks and rakes, and that from the sharp pain in his feet, he guessed he'd broken his ankles.

In the hospital, he was treated by a French doctor with whom he managed to communicate, thanks to the smattering of Portuguese and Crioulo he'd picked up from his parents. His major concern was his legs, for he knew the Germans tended to amputate wounded prisoners as it made them easier to control and transport. But the doctor ended up fixing his ankles with pins before sending him to another town with other prisoners to avoid an Allied bombing. Throughout the journey, Marty worried the Allies would bomb the convoy of Red Cross ambulances, for it was known that the Germans sometimes used them to transport war materials, but the convoy made it to the new hospital unharmed. Then one morning he awoke to find all the guards gone. A few hours later American soldiers arrived to liberate the hospital.

Daddy Grace himself took to his bed on the night of January 7, 1960, age seventy-eight. He felt tired and unwell, and his Berkeley Square bedroom seemed enormous. He asked his butler to bring him a glass of water with sugar, which he drank sitting on the bed while looking at himself in the mirror. Then he asked for his spool tape recorder before dismissing his butler for the night. Daddy Grace picked up the microphone and recorded his final sermon, "You Must Be Born Again."

He suffered a heart attack the next day, and four days later he was dead. At his funeral, loudspeakers pumped out his last words for his followers: "My little bit, your little bit . . . we jealous, oh, bad business children!" His body then traveled from Los Angeles to New Bedford on the Sunset Limited train, stopping off at five cities on the way so that worshippers could bid him farewell.

By then, my great-uncle David had returned to São Nicolau to live out the rest of his days in his house in Caleijão. He died of prostate cancer a few years later, age seventy. He therefore missed, as Grace did, the power struggle for control of the United House of Prayer for All People, a series of disputes over Sweet Daddy's will, and an IRS claim against the estate for $2 million in unpaid taxes.

NINE

Ananias Grosso is a poet whose verses pay homage to the local area and the women, storks, and flatlands that have enriched his life. I visit him at the old people's home in Rio de Moinhos where he lives.

I'm shown into the visitors' room and asked to wait. After a while, Ananias appears at the door on the arm of a nurse. The backdrop of morning sunshine makes it look like he's stepping through a waterfall of light to meet me. His shoulders are gently curved, and he immediately thrusts out a hand, as if greeting an old friend. The hand is a sunbaked ocher color, bony and full of veins like tree roots, the hand of an old man who's known hardship in life. But his gestures suggest he's still full of combative spirit. He moves with assistance, but with purpose and with no sign of the sort of melancholy that sometimes accompanies those who know life is escaping from them. He's wearing a knitted blue cardigan over a black shirt, with black chinos and a black cap. He has a large nose and big ears, and his eyes are gray at the center with blue halos that contrast sharply with the white of his eyeballs.

He apologizes for keeping me waiting, but says he's been a bit fragile since suffering a heart attack on the eve of his ninety-fourth birthday. He makes an expression of disgust at his biological decline, then gives me a fierce stare. I suddenly feel like a bespectacled young anthropologist sitting before a village elder. He makes a dismissive gesture to the nurse, as if to say everything's fine, he can handle me from here.

With the nurse gone, his expression sharpens. He asks me what I want to know about the village, and before I've answered, he starts telling me that the place got its name from a series of five water mills built in a gorge (Rio de Moinhos means "River of Mills" in Portuguese). The water mills were apparently built by people from the nearby village of Alvito who already had some knowledge of them. They'd noticed that the gorge was particularly well suited to water mills and persuaded the owners of the land beside the river to let them build there. Ananias explains the whole process: you find an elevated point in the landscape and build a series of sluices and gates, each one about five hundred meters from the last. There are still two old millstones left, he says, hidden in the bracken somewhere.

I make the most of the pause to ask about Leopoldina. He thinks for a moment, and then I sense a light go on in his memory. "The teacher lady?" he asks, smiling. I nod. "I knew her father and grandfather very well," he says. "Her uncle was a nutter, did you know that? He came back from Africa with some kind of sickness, or so people said at the time. I never liked the bloke."

The man Leopoldina described to me in her notes at the hospital begins to come to life. The local poet, one of the most recognized figures in the region, is a man who knows everyone and knows everyone's stories, even if many of the protagonists are now gone. He's just as I'd hoped he'd be, an old man full of vigor and the gift of the gab, the sort of person who's become accustomed in life to dominating conversations and sucking up all the oxygen in a room. Ananias wasn't born in Rio de Moinhos but in São Romão. He tells me that São Romão was the municipality seat until 1930 and that back then lots of people lived in the two villages, as well as in countless hillside houses and hamlets in between. All the hamlets are empty now, a matter of providence, Ananias says, just like the phenomenon of existence and the meaning of life.

Ananias is everything one might aspire to be in later life: epic in nature, full of vigor and longevity. He has the hawkishness of a bird of prey, able to look down on the world from above, but the humility and loquaciousness of a sparrow. An admirer of the twentieth-century modernist poet José Régio, Ananias has dedicated the latter years of his life to reflecting on the moral and spiritual dimensions of things. In this he is not hindered by being confined to a care home, he says, for it allows him to assess his own vitality. Indeed, he seems so self-assured that I wonder if he combines his lucidity with faith in immortality. He tells me his life is no longer a question of duty and obligation, but adds that life has been surprisingly generous to him, given that he has made such modest personal demands of it.

I ask him what he knows about the populations of Black people who lived in the valley. He ignores the question, telling me instead that he started work at a company owned by his uncle at the age of fifteen, but soon tired of it, and then fell in love. He did his military service in 1939, as part of the Fifth Cavalry in Évora, and after that "led a girl astray" and thought about doing a runner, but didn't. During the Spanish Civil War, people would buy newspapers and give them to him to read out loud. He always lacked the enterprise to work for himself, he admits, but he became a foreman in the rice fields. "The earth was good, you just chucked a handful of rice down and within ninety days there'd be plenty of rice," he recalls. "But the rice fields of today were just reeds back then. The landowner, Dom Rosa Dourado, summoned people from Pinhal Novo, Viseu, and Aveiro, handed out hoes, and had the reeds removed. The workers lived on corn bread with a bit of fish stuffed inside to make a sandwich. There used to be all kinds of fish in the river."

I ask him again if he knew any descendants of Black slaves. Again he ignores me, and I sense he's deliberately evading the question.

"So these people came to break the land to plant rice; it used to be cultivated in a few small patches before that, not widespread across the valley like now. You sowed on the first Friday in March, turning over the soil and watering it. Lots of people came from elsewhere, from the Algarve, for example, to sow and then later to harvest the rice in little sheaves. You dug two or three feet down and planted, and it was ready in no time, you were soon pulling it up. People would put their shoes on the wall and wade out into the water, although most people went around barefoot in those days anyway. The chemicals killed the fish and the bees, but it was amazing really, the way the weed killer destroyed the grass and left the rice. Then it was all carted off, along with the wheat and the cork, four beasts dragging everything down the valley to Porto d'El Rei."

Finally Ananias pauses and fixes me with an enigmatic, ironic expression. He says that everyone writes about the region's Black people in whatever way suits them.

"First there's the malaria story. There used to be a lot of malaria in the region, lots of mosquitoes; I got chronic malaria myself. People ended up yellow from all the quinine. I once had my stomach operated on at Hospital Escolar de Santa Marta in Lisbon, and the doctor asked me why I was so yellow. When I told him where I was from, he said all the quinine they were making us take for malaria was turning us yellow. Then some say it was the Távoras who ordered for Africans to be brought to the region," Ananias continues, referring to an aristocratic family, well known for being stripped of their vast land holdings following an alleged regicide plot in the eighteenth century. "The Africans were brought to Porto d'El Rei by boat, and they remained on the estates afterward and began to work the land. There were whites around too, so they mixed and married and so on. There were a lot in São Mamede, which was an isolated area. So colored men married women from here, that's certainly the case, and a drop of their blood has always remained. You still see colored people around here, with black skin and darky lips and hair and their way of talking, and you see their descendants too, with darky lips and all the rest. The Bacalhaus were a family of coloreds, and the Baiãos, from São Romão. I've a nephew who's a darky, his father was from the Quinta de Cima, which belonged to the Rosa Dourados, and they were all darkies there. When his hair started to grow you saw it, darky hair, exactly the same thickness and color."

Ananias falls silent for a moment, as if to check that my interest in the subject is genuine.

"Older people used to say that the darkies came to teach us how to cultivate rice, which always sounded a bit odd to me, because how could they teach us if they were supposed to be savages? They were forced to break the earth, but the worst of it was when the boat came in full of colored people, and it was awful to see the owners separating families. People say the world is more developed these days, but I'm not so sure. What we had then we have now, just in different ways. It's still slavery, just organized differently. The road that came through here from Beja was paved and the darkies were forced to build it. You still find bits of the road today in some of the estates."

Ananias takes out a white hankie from his pocket and dabs his head. He says that after he became widowed, he turned to poetry and found, in reflecting on the mysteries of life and death and fate, a new companion. Making calculations out loud, he works out that he must have penned some 650 quatrains, spread over dozens of notebooks.

It's almost lunchtime, and I notice the nurse hovering by the door. I get up to leave.

"But don't you want to see our darky?" Ananias suddenly says. "Come on, you can't go without meeting Luísa Baião."

I follow Ananias slowly down the corridor. We pass the lounge and then come to a door. He knocks and we enter. An old lady is sitting propped up in bed. Her skin is dark, her face covered in pale blotches the size of coins. At ninety-six, she's the oldest woman in the home and, indeed, the village. When she sees us, she looks at us blankly and uneasily, but Ananias approaches her and says something reassuring in her ear. She stares at me with sad, confused eyes, but then suddenly her expression changes and a smile lights up her face, as if she's seen some kind of revelation in me. With a heavy gesture, infused with unshakable dignity, she points me to a chair. I sit down eagerly: her story promises to be fascinating and moving. I have to contain myself, and I make an effort to speak calmly and clearly.

Alas, despite her friendliness and goodwill, her deafness proves an insurmountable obstacle. She's reached an age where the voices she hears and the sounds that reach her most clearly may not be of this world. From what little I'm able to garner, I learn that she, like her brothers and sisters, worked for her whole life on the Quinta de Cima and Herdade da Salema estates. She tells me that workers also came from Pegões, Benavente, and the Algarve to pull up the rice in the month of São João. That's all we manage. We admit defeat with honest, gracious smiles, her countless unknown stories left untold. We say farewell with a wordless whisper of life.

Back out in the corridor, Ananias reminds me that dark, swarthy people like Luísa Baião and her brothers and sisters even spoke a different language, using words like *lingriça* and *vrido* (*lingriça* for *linguiça*, meaning "sausage"; *vrido* for *vidro*, meaning "glass"). I leave the place with the vague idea of compiling a dictionary of words used by the "crossbreeds," a project that would have no doubt pleased Leite de Vasconcelos. The habits, colors, and sounds that propagated these riverways seem destined to fade, but perhaps the lexicon might be preserved, the slang and the slights of everyday life.

Ananias waves me off at the main door, and I wonder how I will remember him, this world-weary, evasive old man; this self-appointed custodian of his people's culture, accidental historian, and cynic. A man who found, in poetry, a way to reshape reason and history, and a means to transcend the smallness of his little village in the Sado valley.

The Rosa Dourados established themselves in the region in the early twentieth century. Their Quinta de Cima estate once covered 1,100 hectares, though it has now been split in two. The most developed half belongs to an agriculture company, while the other half is the subject of a dispute among eight inheritors.

I set off up the hill toward the estate's assembly of buildings, keeping to the shade thrown by a row of oaks that flank the dirt track. A Renault Clio comes down the hill toward me. It stops, and the driver introduces himself as the son of the caretaker couple who look after what remains of the estate. He waves me on my way and continues on his.

A little farther on I see the couple: a man in his seventies is driving a tractor with a trailer laden with cork, while a woman shouts instructions. On the other side of the wall are modern facilities that look like warehouses or silos for grain, but on this side the buildings are mostly in ruins, especially those that presumably once housed the workers. They are arranged around a yard like a miniature rectangular village, but their walls have tumbled to the ground as if bombed.

Ducks and chickens come running out of crude wooden sheds to investigate me. I walk on up through an olive grove. From slightly higher ground, I'm able to look down over what would have been the master's house. The roof has caved in and lies collapsed on the veranda. It must have made quite a crash when it fell. I can see into the main living room, where the Rosa Dourados would have received guests, served tea in china cups with silver spoons, perhaps danced to music on the gramophone. Considering the gaping hole in the roof, the floor tiles and wooden paneling look to be in pretty good nick. But these days a family of storks are the real masters of the house.

I carry on walking up the hill for a few hours, winding through cork trees and stone pines. I keep an eye out for the paved road Ananias mentioned but see no sign of it. Eventually the Vale do Gaio dam comes into view. I keep going and reach a cobbled road that runs along the top of the dam, leading to a luxury hotel on the far side of the reservoir. The water level looks pretty low. The valley spreads out before me, lushly green and placidly melancholic. A narrow road descends into a pine forest to the right, snaking out of sight. It's a muggy afternoon, but the forest looks cool. I decide to go and see where the road leads.

I discover a series of connected water basins and, a moment or two later, realize I've reached the source of the irrigation canal system. It's not quite a river spring, but it seems like the logical conclusion to my Sado valley journey. I feel satisfied but a little bit downcast too. I tell myself that there's poetry in any kind of spring, and, being from Cape Verde, where periodic droughts have brought devastation, I understand the importance of water management. The reservoir fills the basins, which feed the sluices that spread life through the valley: it's all part of the life cycle, the possibility of plenitude, the assurance that it is never too late.

Back near the top of the dam, I see a Datsun pickup truck parked under the trees. I hear a splash in the water and look down over some rocks toward the reservoir. A man with a fishing rod stands on the shore. He reels in his line and throws it out again, achieving impressive distance. A few minutes later he gets a bite. The fish struggles to the surface, but the man calmly draws the catch in. I watch him for a while, then hit the road back to Rio de Moinhos.

The next morning, I place the house key on the sideboard in the hall, as agreed, and leave early to catch the seven A.M. bus to Grândola. From there I will take a train south to the Algarve. My Sado expedition has come to an end, but I feel my journey will be complete only once I've seen the port where the first enslaved Africans arrived.

VIII

One morning when I was eight, two years after we'd moved to Portugal, I was sent out to buy bread and found the air thick with the smell of burning. A few blocks on, I came across an area the size of a soccer field that had burned to cinders. Firemen in little blue helmets pointed hoses at the destruction, snuffing out the last plumes of smoke. Other firefighters, looking visibly exhausted, smoked and chatted with policemen. Farther back, a crowd had gathered to gawk and gossip about how quickly the fire had spread. Those who'd watched the fire unfold from the windows and balconies of surrounding buildings drew the attention of latecomers like me, their eyewitness accounts prompting a mixture of awe and incredulity.

Such fires were widely feared and regularly warned of by the emergency services, a danger associated with the overuse of gas cylinders in Lisbon's shantytowns. They were also epic events, visual and emotional spectacles. What had been, the previous day, a dense community of huts beside the fish market was now a bed of ashes, carbonized wood, and twisted metal.

On the other side of the train track, entire families sat on chairs beside wooden tables piled high with salvaged items: rolled-up mattresses, fold-out camping beds, suitcases, wicker baskets stuffed with pillows, saucepans, bowls, cooking stoves, coats. A steady flow of new arrivals dumped more items on the ground. Three men went by carrying a heavy wardrobe on their backs. I saw an elderly woman holding a baby sitting on a bedside table beside a wall mirror that reflected the devastating scene behind me. The woman emanated a strange sense of calm. Clearly, fires and catastrophes were part and parcel of life. Two little boys and a freckled girl played happily among the mattresses and boxes.

Like everyone else, I looked on in compassionate silence. I had no idea what would happen to these people, but I told myself that they were surely waiting for relatives to come and pick them up, and the thought pleased me. But I never saw them again. The shacks that didn't burn were knocked down not long afterward, and the site became an empty lot, abandoned except for when a fair came to town or when a circus tent was raised at Christmas.

I'd always felt bad for the families who lived in wooden shacks with corrugated iron roofs near us. Going down labyrinthine passageways that tunneled into the hearts of these neighborhoods, I was drawn to them out of a mixture of fear and adventure. I felt an irrepressible urge to establish bonds of friendship with the kids my age, stigmatized by the muddy streets they called home. I suppose my efforts to play games and share secrets with them were an attempt to prove that they were not, as people said, inherently wicked.

But other than stirring up a bit of prejudice, these shantytowns seemed to make little impression on anyone. The city authorities didn't appear to care about the deplorable state these people lived in, and the locals behaved as if it was just one of those things that was nobody's fault. Such neighborhoods could only have existed in a place where extreme poverty was deeply entrenched, yet for an immigrant like me, a child of the Portuguese empire, it was hard to marry with the tales of greatness—voyages of discovery; a vast and glorious civilization—on which I'd been educated.

This was the early 1970s, a time when independence for Portugal's so-called overseas provinces still seemed a long way off, and these people were living in the metropole, the capital of the empire. They had life stories very similar to ours. We were all part of the same mass movement of the world's disenfranchised to the big cities. We had come from overseas more recently, while they had come to Lisbon from Portugal's rural interior two or three generations back. It was hard not to think about how much more successful our migration story had been.

In the early 1960s, rural poverty brought Portuguese families to the cities, but by the end of the decade, Cape Verdeans had started to arrive to fill a labor shortage. Independence movements in Angola, Mozambique, and Guinea-Bissau turned into the Colonial Wars with Cold War components and national service for Portuguese men, increased to four years in 1967, with two of them to be spent on tours of duty in Africa. This took scores of young men away from home for long periods of time. While many, of course, never came back, others fled Portugal to avoid the draft, typically heading to France or the United States. Cape Verdean men, escaping drought and hardship themselves, were drawn to Portugal by the possibility of manual work. Come 1974 and Portugal's April 25 Revolution, a postcolonial, post-dictatorship world brought more migration. Lisbon's shantytowns became melting pots for displaced Portuguese, Africans, and Romani.

The Alto de Santa Catarina neighborhood outside Algés, at Lisbon's western city limits, is now a plush area of condominium tower blocks. However, its name derives from a shantytown built by Cape Verdean laborers from Santa Catarina, on Santiago. *Alto* means "high," and the place offers magnificent views of the Tejo Estuary.

The Santa Catarina settlers were construction workers by day who put their building and carpentry skills to use in their spare time, raising a neighborhood for themselves to live in almost from one day to the next. They put up walls, tiled roofs, and cemented access paths. Next they built amenities, in particular bars and cafés where they could relax from their construction jobs on the weekends. On Sundays they'd organize communal lunches, and friends and family would come to visit; I remember Nho António Silvério, Dona Cucha, and Senhor Manelóna heartily hosting us several times. They'd lived their whole lives in the countryside of the islands, far away from big cities, and although they'd emigrated, they brought the same sense of serenity and respect for their elders to their new surroundings. Their hilltop island of wood, brick, and zinc grew fast, and I can imagine the look of satisfaction on the original members' faces. Not only had they managed to forge their own piece of home in a new city—no small achievement—but they'd done so in a place where they could see the Atlantic, the better to recall friends and family farther south.

But a sea view was not the only similarity with the houses they'd left behind in Cape Verde. Their new dwellings had no running water and open sewers, just like back home, and electricity was commandeered from the nearest pylon. Men got drunk, beat their wives, brawled, and even stabbed each other on particularly raucous Saturday nights, though by day their energy went into improving their homes or helping others do so. Every so often, a land registry agent would show up to remind them where they were and that they weren't exempt from the country's laws. But by then there were so many "informal" neighborhoods the authorities knew they were fighting a losing battle.

The Alto de Santa Catarina shantytown hugged the Estrada Militar (Military Road), a ring road built around Lisbon in the late nineteenth century, mirroring the curve of the river. Originally used to move troops and weapons, the Estrada Militar was rendered obsolete by the emergence of airplanes in World War

I. By the mid-1960s, it no longer served any military purpose at all and became a public wasteland. When Cape Verdean families came along and built huts for homes, no one cared or even gave the matter much thought. The eastern stretch of the road made way for Portela Airport in the 1940s, but sections of the western end still exist today. From Alto de Santa Catarina, the road winds northeast before being swallowed up by the urban hub of Queluz, then resurfacing around the back of Amadora. The old city gates at Portas de Benfica, freshly painted pink like a fairy-tale castle, now occupy a giant grassy roundabout, but used to be surrounded by the Bairro das Fontainhas shantytown. Indeed, the whole area from the gates down to the Damaia train station was claimed by waves of Cape Verdeans and remains home to many today. Behind the Cova da Moura and Buraca neighborhoods lies Bairro de 6 de Maio, or what's left of it. Deemed a problem area by the police, the architecture here is chaotic and poverty is conspicuous. Mismanaged rehousing schemes have left people hanging around, waiting outside bars for their turn to move or wandering the streets like ghosts. Along the train track toward Damaia-Reboleira, makeshift houses have only recently been abandoned, with piles of litter and discarded building materials left behind.

Heading east through Pontinha and Bairro Padre Cruz, the old Estrada Militar has been superseded by the CRIL/IC-17, a beltway that runs almost parallel to the old ring road. Built in the 1990s and 2000s, the new road displaced several informal housing communities. The Estrada Militar carries on all the same, passing through country fields and social housing projects at Lumiar before being cut off by the Calçada de Carriche freeway and the airport. The last vestiges of former shantytowns still dot the landscape. Rehousing schemes have been only partially successful, with some residents resentful of the forced displacement. Condemned houses lie abandoned but still standing, while others show signs of life, satellite dishes on roofs or grilles on windows, evidence of inhabitants who have stood their ground. This uncoordinated exodus has resulted in some houses being demolished while neighboring homes remain standing. Those that had two stories leave layers of wallpaper or tiles on adjoining walls, as if they've been cut out like a slice of cake. Others look as if they've been hit by a missile.

The Estrada Militar reemerges around the back of the airport on the approach to the neighborhood of Fetais. As a byway, it serves practically no purpose and is mostly used by builders who dump rubble at the roadside. The road ends at Camarate, where, in recent years, new shantytowns have sprung up.

TEN

And my eyes slowly close as I succumb to the lure of sleep. The rocking of the train lulls me, and most curtains in the carriage are drawn to keep out the sunlight. My thoughts slow down, and I recall the last conversation I had with Leopoldina's niece. She told me her aunt was okay, that her condition was "stationary," as the doctors put it, which makes her sound like a parked car waiting to be driven away. But the main thing is she's still lucid. She likely won't be allowed to live on her own again when she comes out of the hospital, meaning she'll move in with her niece. I smile as I imagine visiting her there and sharing all the details of my trip.

Then suddenly my subconscious stirs, alerted to the sound of Crioulo voices. I turn to see two mixed-race women in their fifties sitting behind me on the train, chatting away about a friend's daughter's wedding: the church, the guest list, the flower arrangements, the costs. Then they suddenly switch to Dutch to address two children sitting across the aisle, a boy and a girl, both blond and blue-eyed. A middle-aged couple sitting opposite them, looking out the window at the Algarve countryside, appear to be the children's parents. It takes me a few moments to interpret the scene, but it seems that two Cape Verdean nannies are on holiday with their employers.

I'm transported to my own childhood, when Dutch guilders transformed São Nicolau. New houses with terraces were built all over Ribeira Grande by immigrants to the Netherlands or their families, rich on remittance payments. In the 1960s, Rotterdam was the largest port in the world and countless young men from Cape Verde went there seeking work. Demand was high and international ships were always recruiting for crew, making it relatively easy to get a job. A support network built up around the docks, with Cape Verdean–run guesthouses to stay in, old-timers looking out for new arrivals, and friends forever summoning fresh recruits.

If work-hungry Cape Verdean men headed to the Netherlands, their female counterparts made for Italy. Scores of Cape Verdean women were employed as housemaids in Italy, a consequence of church exchanges, Alitalia connections, and a snowball effect. Eventually the two strands combined, with Cape Verdean men persuading their sisters to join them in the Netherlands, where they claimed pay and conditions were better.

I listen to the way the two women on the train speak Dutch, capturing the guttural Rs of "Rembrandt" and "Vermeer." They're unlikely to have been educated beyond primary school in Cape Verde, yet their command of a Germanic language has not only secured them a job of great trust but also made them so indispensable or loved that they have accompanied the family on vacation. Their presence, and the purpose of my trip to the Algarve, brings another Dutch speaker to mind. By mastering Dutch and Latin, Jacobus Capitein was able to defend and publish his university thesis, a remarkable achievement for a boy from Africa sold into slavery at age seven. The fact that his thesis was a defense of slavery remains mystifying to this day.

The boy who became Jacobus Elisa Johannes Capitein was born in 1717 in what is now Ghana. The area had first been colonized by the Portuguese but was by then controlled by the Dutch, who operated a number of trading posts, including a major slaving port run out of Elmina fort. Arnold Steenhard, a Dutch captain, bought the boy and, ignoring his African name, took to calling him Capitein, Dutch for "captain." But Steenhard soon tired of owning a boy and ended up giving him to Jacob van Goch, a colleague at the Dutch West India Company. When Van Goch opted to return to the Netherlands, Capitein's destiny changed forever.

Like Portugal, the Netherlands encouraged the transatlantic slave trade but made it illegal to bring a slave into the country: when Van Goch's ship entered Middelburg, just south of Rotterdam, Capitein became a free man. Van Goch took Capitein to live with him in The Hague and gave him a privileged education, which began with him learning the language and the catechism. A bright boy, Capitein came to the attention of a number of teachers and sponsors who smoothed the way to his enrollment at the Latin School of The Hague, followed by admission to Leiden University to study theology. At age eighteen, Capitein experienced what he would describe as the most important moment of his life when he was baptized by his former catechism teacher in the presence of the three people he loved the most: Jacob van Goch, his adopted father; Elizabeth van Goch, Jacob's sister and a mother figure to him; and Johanna Mulder, Jacob van Goch's niece, Capitein's closest friend and a fledgling love interest. As a show of gratitude, he adopted all their names and became Jacobus Elisa Johannes Capitein.

Seven years later, an assembly of professors and worthies gave Capitein a standing ovation at Leiden University after he argued that slavery was perfectly compatible with Christian values. Ordained as a pastor (*predikant* in Dutch) shortly thereafter, his defense of slavery made him, in the eyes of the Dutch Reformed Church, an ideal candidate for missionary work in Africa. In 1742, he began his journey back to Elmina.

Capitein seems to have expected to be met with acclaim on his return. The portraits he had commissioned to accompany the publication of his thesis, a book that went through four print runs in its first year, give some indication of Capitein's sense of pride. In all of them he sports a curly-haired wig, typical of the eighteenth century, and a gown befitting a scholar and a cleric. His round cheeks and double chin give him a jovial air, but also show him to be no stranger to the pleasures of the table. In one picture, he stands before a bookcase holding a Bible, while in another he points to a passage with one hand and to his chest with the other, as if to say, *Look, herein lies my destiny*. For all their pomposity, the images also subvert the artistic conventions of portraiture at the time: here is an African man, with black skin and typical African features, yet he is not a servant or dressed for caricature; rather, he is evidently the equal of his peers.

Capitein was genuinely enthused by his evangelizing mission, eager to be useful to his people and to help the heathen find their way out of the darkness. But the devil was in the details, for in Capitein's view, which formed the basis of his thesis, spiritual liberty was not to be confused with physical liberty. The New and Old Testaments are both ambiguous in their messages about slavery: Capitein's stance naturally required him to willfully ignore certain passages. His argument was based around the idea that freedom and slavery are spiritual rather than bodily concepts. In particular, he claimed that true freedom was freedom from sin.

Like many Protestant defenders of slavery, Capitein harked back to the Curse of Ham in the book of Genesis: Ham finds his father, Noah, lying naked and drunk, and makes fun of him, earning his father's ire; Noah puts a curse on Ham's son, Canaan, as punishment, condemning him and all his future descendants to lives of servitude. Some clerics claimed that Africans were the predestined sons of Ham, even that the curse was the root cause of blackness itself. Capitein stopped short of this, merely arguing that the curse was the origin of slavery, and that if God had allowed slavery to come into existence, it surely featured in his plans.

The fort at Elmina had been built as the São Jorge da Mina Castle by the Portuguese, who named the area the Gold Coast, having first traded for gold there, before switching to ivory, pepper, and people. As a slave post, the fort was used as a depot to house prisoners caught and brought from elsewhere in West Africa. There was a marketplace where the enslaved were auctioned, as well as cells, originally built to store goods, where they were kept in filthy, airless, overcrowded conditions. Two cells were set aside for disciplinary purposes, one for errant members of the garrison, the other for runaway slaves and subversives, who were starved to death then thrown out to sea as an example to others. Another sea exit was the "Door of No Return," a single-file corridor that led from the cells straight out to boats that ferried slaves to bigger ships waiting in the bay.

Above the cells, on the first floor, were quarters for the garrison, Dutch West India Company employees, and visiting traders. At one end was the chaplain's room, where Capitein lived; at the other, the superintendent's chambers. The upper floor belonged to the director general, who ran the castle and the Dutch West India Company's Gold Coast operations.

On the other side of the yard was a church built by the Portuguese, a barn, and the women's cells. The director general had only to appear on his balcony and give the order, and the female slaves were brought out and paraded in the yard. He would point at one, and she would be washed at the cistern and given something to eat, then led up a side stairway to his bedroom. After being abused by the director general, the woman would often then be raped by several soldiers before being dumped back in the cells.

Capitein found his mission as chaplain of the fort impossible. Members of the garrison and the company did not take kindly to being told to mend their ways, while the slaves themselves, and the Black population at large, did not see the *predikant* as one of them. He wrote a letter to his superiors in Amsterdam, asking for permission to marry a young African woman in order to win the trust and affections of the local people. His request was vetoed on the grounds that such a woman would have to be baptized and that he was the only person authorized to do it; he could not both baptize and marry someone.

Accepting that he was powerless to stop the endless flow of biracial babies being born within the fort and the town, Capitein turned his attention to evangelizing the children instead. In this his problems were more practical than theological, and this inspired the linguist in him. He worked hard to recover his lost mother tongue, and with the help of a learned old African who lived in the fort, he translated the Ten Commandments, the Lord's Prayer, and the Twelve Articles of Faith into Fante. But when he sent his efforts back to the Netherlands for printing, his superiors in the Dutch Reformed Church were outraged. They disapproved of his failure to consult them on the initiative and of the liberties he'd taken with the translation: in a preface, Capitein explained the need to switch words such as "donkey," an animal the people of Elmina had never seen before, to the more familiar "horse."

This last rebuke proved something of a final straw for Capitein, coming on the back of his numerous ignored appeals for assistance and improved conditions. He carried on evangelizing in his mother tongue regardless, but his relationship with Amsterdam never recovered and he increasingly sought solace in wine. He died in February 1747, age thirty, heavily in debt and disillusioned, the cause of his death and the location of his tomb unknown.

The train starts to empty out as we enter the Algarve, as passengers get off to head for the resorts. Locals replace the tourists and linger by the doors with bicycles and produce to sell at the market. We pass sumptuous summer houses with brash marble columns and ornamental trees, fig and carob tree groves with brick-colored soil, orange orchards thriving in the rolling hills. As we approach Faro, I think of Samuel and his odyssey as a former slave. The journey I have just made by train, he covered entirely on foot.

The Cape Verdean nannies have fallen quiet, the Dutch children fallen to sleep. I turn my head and see the mother and father sitting in silence, watching the world go by. Their fair hair catches the late-morning sunlight, and framed by the window, they look like an Edward Hopper painting. The scene suits my wistfulness, and I recall another African, thirteen years older than Capitein, who returned to the Gold Coast the same year the *predikant* died. Their lives traced remarkably similar arcs, but Anton Wilhelm Amo's thoughts on slavery couldn't have been more different.

Born in 1703 in Axim, modern-day Ghana, Amo was likewise taken to the Netherlands as a child by employees of the Dutch West India Company. Unlike Capitein, however, he is not thought to have been a slave: it's understood that his parents put him in the care of the company so he could gain an education and religious training. The company struggled to find a foster family for the child in the Netherlands, so presented him to Anthony Ulrich, a German duke, in Amsterdam. The duke agreed to take him in and gave him to his son, August Wilhelm. Amo was taken to Wolfenbüttel in Lower Saxony, Germany, where he was baptized and given the name of his new guardians.

Why the Duke of Brunswick-Wolfenbüttel adopted Amo is unclear, but it has been noted that the duke was related by marriage to Peter the Great, with whom he shared Enlightenment ideas. The czar adopted his own Black African boy, Abraham Petrovitch Gannibal, around the same time.

If we know few details of Amo's early life, it is because, unlike Capitein, whose thesis began with an autobiographical account, he left no written record of his background or any portraits. His writings were almost exclusively concerned with philosophy. What little we know about his early life comes from the diary notes of David Henri Gallandet, a Swiss-Dutch naval surgeon who met Amo in Axim in 1753.

Amo's life as a young man is better documented. He read law at Halle University and gained a master's in philosophy and the liberal arts at Wittenberg University. He also studied languages, medicine, physiology, and psychology and went on to become a professor of philosophy, teaching first at Halle and later at Jena University. As a philosopher, he was acclaimed for his work on the human mind. He argued against Descartes's notion of mind-body dualism, saying that while it was possible to talk about body and mind separately, it was the body that both perceived and felt.

This view contrasts with Capitein's belief in the freedom of the sprit as distinct from that of the body. Indeed, Amo's philosophical studies led him to reject clericalism outright and to embrace humanism and freethinking. His law dissertation at Halle, entitled "The Rights of Moors in Europe," denounced slavery. He made his argument not on moral grounds but on the basis that it was against the law, or at least Roman law, which most European countries professed to honor. He showed that Africa had been considered a province of the Roman Empire and that, as former Roman citizens, Africans had therefore inherited the same legacy rights and privileges as their European counterparts. He was making a legal point but also an intellectual argument that appealed to the spirit of reason so beloved of his Enlightenment peers.

By 1743, Amo's various academic sponsors and mentors had all died, with Anthony Ulrich and August Wilhelm long gone. It is not known precisely why he returned to Africa, but a lack of financial and moral support seems likely. After being reunited with relatives at Axim, he quickly acquired a reputation for being a sage among his people, prompting the visiting Gallandet to seek him out.

According to the doctor, Amo later went to live at the San Sebastian Fort in Shama, which was operated by the Dutch West India Company. It's hard to imagine that he willfully chose to leave the village he lived in with his father and sister in order to take up residence in a fort surrounded by Dutch slavers. More plausibly, the Dutch authorities feared the impact his intellect and ideas might have on the local population and their lucrative trade in human trafficking. At any rate, nothing more is known of Amo.

Like Elmina, the San Sebastian Fort was originally built by the Portuguese. The two trading posts–cum–slaving warehouses, just thirty miles apart, still stand today, open to the public as national monuments and visitor sites. I'm on my way to see another one, the former slave market at Lagos.

IX

My stepfather died without realizing he was dying (as we all hope to, in a manner of speaking). The decisive moment came when he was completely anesthetized to the cold by the amount of alcohol he'd consumed that night—the ironies of fate for a man accustomed to the rigors of a north European winter.

My mum had seen very little of him in recent times. She occasionally spotted him out and about, crossing the road very slowly, for example, as if he doubted his ability to get to the other side. Or as if getting there was of but minor interest to him. She would call out to him and he'd pretend not to hear, even when they both knew he must have seen her coming from the top of the road. Sometimes she'd invite him back to the house for a bowl of soup or a cup of coffee. He almost always said he'd already eaten or just had a hot drink. If she insisted, he might yield and struggle up the four flights of stairs to her flat. She'd serve him at the table, talking to him. But she gradually came to realize that he was either going deaf or mostly on another planet. Afterward, she'd ask him if he needed anything, if he had enough money. She knew he did have money because his bank statements still went to her and his pension was paid into his account by a shipping company in Germany every month. But still, she asked him how much money he had because she didn't trust the company he kept, single men, unemployed bums for the most part, who she suspected ate and drank on his account. But he barely ever said a word in reply.

My younger brother would also look out for him in the neighborhood bars and take him to spend weekends with him. He'd buy him new clothes and make him wash, then take him for drives to the local tourist spots. But as he told me over the phone once, our stepdad had become increasingly "distant." He took longer and longer to understand what was being said to him. Silence became his ever more constant comfort zone. My mum said she often found herself crying when she watched him disappearing down the street.

I catch the ferry from Lisbon to Almada to go and meet an old seafarer who'd been like a brother to my stepfather. During the short river crossing, I try to get my thoughts in order. I know that if I really want to understand my stepfather's life, I need to look beyond my memories of him.

I remember my uncles talking about the pretty women they met in ports all over the world. They kept photos of their favorite Asian "muses" or described them so well I can still picture them, high heels clattering down the pavement, broad smiles, breathtaking availability. In many ways, my stepfather's generation had it lucky: sailors and men of the world, parts of crews that were white, Black, blond, Latino, Asian—mostly Filipino. They would dock in different ports and be astonished to find themselves amid such an explosion of life, to be where the sun came up before it did anywhere else in the world. My uncles told stories of dazzling restaurants and having to learn new ways of doing things; it was as if they entered another dimension every time they docked. The cities of the Far East were generous to those who disembarked at their ports and breathed in their air, offering quick, cheap, exotic thrills: "Hello, baby, looking for good time?"

The sailors must have been awestruck by this promise of love at an unknown latitude, proffered under neon signs, surrounded by the sounds of ambulance and police sirens, a night breeze delivering smells of spicy fast food. Some of the men would still have had traces of oil and detergent under their nails, the rudimentary shower of the ship's cabin unable to entirely remove these telltale signs. Their clothes would have clung to their bodies, unaccustomed to the high humidity.

Surely this was where true life was to be experienced: bright lights that defied the blackness of night; conversations spoken in quick, mysterious tongues; women with dolls' faces who would whisper suggestive words in their ears, words that would echo in their minds during their many months at sea, traveling the world on cargo ships and oil tankers, increasing the wealth of nations.

There's a picture in one of our family photo albums of my stepfather dressed dashingly in a shiny beige shirt with gold cuffs, surrounded by a motley crew of other foreign sailors. He was a lively, headstrong boy from a village on São Vicente who sailed the oceans and saw more of the world than most men of his age. He and his fellow seamen all answered the same call: to live a little, to taste life in all its fragile extremes. Come rain or shine, they would never feel so alive and full of hope as they did as twenty-somethings in Kobe, Yokohama, Fukushima, Singapore, Port Klang, Shanghai, Yangzhou, or Hong Kong, experiencing one revelation after another. There was no time to think about death; you went with the flow, riding the waves and your luck, though some perhaps assigned a certain metaphysical aura to their fate.

Juca retired from seafaring many years ago. He ushers me into the living room and motions for me to sit on a brown leather sofa. A giant photo on the wall shows the main square in Ribeira Brava, his hometown on São Nicolau. Smaller framed photos sit atop various items of furniture. Most are of his wife and kids, but one shows three young men on the deck of an oil tanker: two of the men are bare-chested and look as if they're going through some sort of boxing routine under the tutelage of the third.

Juca begins by telling me about one evening in Rotterdam in the early 1960s, when he bumped into Pio, as he calls my stepfather, in a bar called Le Ciel Bleu that was popular with Cape Verdean immigrants at the time. My father exclaimed, "They might as well close the doors right now, Juca, because tonight we're the only customers in town!" But then Juca confides in me that Pio was a man with more than one personality.

They first met in 1952 at the Escola da Pontinha, a vocational college on São Vicente. They became good friends, but not immediately: "We were twelve or thirteen and the two cockiest kids in class, just spoiling for a fight," says Juca. "Then one day your father says, 'Juca, we've nothing to fight about! Let's join forces and go and kick some ass over there instead.'"

According to Juca, Pio was tough but nimble, adept at making things like locks and needles for lacework. He says Pio was one of the best students at the college, which was run by a legendary figure named Teodoro "Kunk" Gomes, a man committed to making sure every young man on São Vicente gained sufficient workshop skills to earn an apprenticeship at one of the foreign-run machine shops or filling stations on the island, or indeed in the engine room of a ship docked in Rotterdam.

"Back then, our parents didn't have the means to send us to school, so we went to Pontinha to become apprentices. Your father was placed with Shell, and I always went with him when he got his lunch, because he'd give me whatever he could spare."

Juca moved to Dakar, and they didn't see each other for a while, until my stepfather followed him to Senegal. "We met at a nightclub called Sefa, in Gueule Tapée, where we danced the cha-cha-cha all night. Pio loved the cha-cha-cha!"

In 1956, Juca set sail on the *Casamance*, a steamship owned by the French shipping company Compagnie Nationale de Navigation. "I tried to get Pio a place alongside me in the kitchen, but he wanted to work in the engine room. Then not long after that I found out he'd taken a job as a cook on the *Peter Hess*, a Dutch boat."

Their paths soon crossed again, in Curaçao and Aruba, in the Dutch Antilles. As ever, their reunions were full of party spirit. "We danced the twist, the salsa, the cumbia—the port guys always sorted us out with some chicks from Bonaire, who we could get along well with speaking in Papiamento. Pio would say, 'Oh, Juca, if only we could stop the hands on the clock right now . . .' Another time, I bumped into him in Lisbon, at the Andaluz nightclub—it must have been the early 1980s—at this big party for the crew of an Esso Netherlands supertanker. We hugged and almost cried with joy when we saw each other that night."

Through the course of our conversation, I find out Juca also knew my uncle Simão and that they traveled to the Netherlands together by train from Lisbon.

"In the early 1960s, a few of us Cape Verdeans were lodged at number 152 Rua do Poço dos Negros, in Lisbon, in a first-floor flat owned by Dona Joaquina, Nho Damatinha's sister. In February 1963, a group of us—me, your uncle, Zinzin Santiago, Junior, Vicente, and "Bad" Toi Lopes—set off from there, each with his own knapsack, and caught the train at Santa Apolónia. We were trying to get to Holland. We had to change trains at Hendaye, and we all went to buy provisions, but none of them spoke any French, and when we got back to the station, I saw how they'd all been ripped off in the local shops. I had to go back with them to get them their change, and I told the shopkeepers, '*Vous n'avez pas fait bonne service avec mes copains . . .*' Your uncle Simão was gobsmacked by my French."

Juca and my uncle continued as colleagues afterward on a Dutch cargo ship called the *Vieness*, making twenty-one-day trips around Europe.

"There was a Corsican boatswain who used to go down the corridor waking the European sailors up with a gentle knock. When he got to the Cape Verdean cabins, he hammered right where he knew our heads were in the bunks. I told everyone, 'Don't worry, I'll knock some sense into him.' So one day, in Hamburg, I was waiting for him when he did it and I socked him one right there; '*Pourquoi vous me frappez comme ça?*' he said. But that night he gave me a bottle of gin that the officers drank as an aperitif and that we, the deckhands, were not entitled to. Then he turned to me with an *everything cool with us now?* expression. Your uncle asked me, '*Já bo coçal oss?*' [a Crioulo expression, roughly meaning 'You had a bone to pick with him, right?'] No one ever mistreated a Cape Verdean if I was around. The day I left the company, the captain said to me, 'Think about what you're doing, because if I hand the papers you've just signed over to the bosses, we're losing our best cook, but your guys are losing a leader.' By then I was a chief steward, one of the first Cape Verdeans to gain a cooking diploma from a Dutch company. My opinion was always considered important to the captain.

"Once in the Pacific," Juca continued, "on a trip from Sakai to Melbourne, we hit bad weather in northern Japan—our normal speed was eighteen miles an hour, but we didn't even manage to move five miles in twenty-four hours because of a storm, and in the middle of it our radiotelegraphist got an SOS from a boat forty miles away. We went to rescue them. The captain called for me and asked if there was enough food in the dispensary for seven more men. I said, 'Don't worry, we've still got five more days to go, but we'll sort something out.'"

Besides being in charge of the dispensary, Juca often served as an interpreter: he spoke Italian, Spanish, French, Greek, Wolof, and English as well as Portuguese and Creole. "Wherever we docked, I was always the one sent to buy provisions, even in places like the Soviet Union, where it was very hard to get fresh supplies."

While Juca talks, I think about my father's spendthrift attitude. I begin to understand that unmistakable look of self-assurance in the family photo album.

"The likes of me and Pio saw more of the world than most men of our generation. We tended to prefer the Americas, because it was easier in terms of language, music, food, women, et cetera. But the country that made the biggest impression on me was Japan. People there would leave their shoes at the door of their own homes, but also to go into dance halls. I must have been to at least twenty cities in Japan, and I never saw a calmer people. They never ran. Once, in Osaka, a siren went off to say a typhoon was coming, but no one broke out into a run. New Zealand and

Australia were also very impressive; we would go there to pick up a cargo of onions to take back to Holland. The onions were transported in special crates, and for several days of the journey the hold had to be left open. Whenever it rained, a cloud of flies emerged from the onions and almost ate us alive. In Australia, I once saw a policeman stop the traffic to let some crustaceans cross the road. Then there was Canada, where we traveled up the Saint Lawrence River as far as Detroit and Duluth, an amazing trip."

Juca's sad expression laments my stepfather's demise.

"Pio was a good person when he didn't drink. He was a peaceful soul when there was no alcohol involved, believe you me. And I know what I'm talking about: if I hadn't decided to retire, on January 20, 1980, I might not be alive today either."

Having contemplated the end, Juca goes back to the beginning.

"When we started out as apprentices in the dockyards on São Vicente in the 1950s, there was a special motorboat that took oil out to ships anchored in the bay. No matter how hard we worked the motor, the boat would only ever start when it felt like it. We nicknamed it Tont Ta Dam. And that was Pio's motto in life." *Tont ta dam*: Crioulo for "Don't give a damn."

Before bidding me farewell, Juca makes a point of showing me an inflatable dinghy he keeps on the balcony. It has red-and-white plastic flowers inside it and was bought in Tokyo in 1964.

ELEVEN

A narrow street flanked by one- and two-story white houses. A group of seven children playing on the cobbles in the sun. Across the street, in the shade, a boy sits on a wooden bench looking up at a woman in a black headscarf; she's holding a baby and perhaps talking to someone inside the house. In the background, farther down the street, two men are chatting with another man, who lingers by the seven children with his head turned.

But the image is dominated by a statuesque woman standing with one arm pressed against the wall. Her bright face seems to draw in all the light and she's staring right at us, straight into the camera lens.

The photo is by Artur Pastor and comes from a book called *As mulheres do meu país* (*The Women of My Country*), a collection of pictures he took while touring the country with his Rolleiflex in the 1940s. Written texts by Maria Lamas accompany Pastor's photos.

This one is a scene of daily life in Barreta, a fishing neighborhood in Olhão, a town in the Algarve. I've stopped off in Olhão to see if I can track down any of Miquinha de Djena's relations. Miquinha was an old friend of my mother's who left Pedra de Lume, on Sal, in 1967, after securing a place on an Algarvian trawler. He ended up settling in Olhão and starting a family. I remember him coming to our house in Lisbon several times. He was a man with an affable smile and a happy-go-lucky attitude. He used to take me and my little brother to the candy store and tell us to choose whatever we wanted—a gesture guaranteed to win a child's affections for life. But he was popular with everyone, so it was a great shock when he disappeared at sea just a few months shy of retirement.

Miquinha was a fisherman from Cape Verde who made his home among the fishermen of the Algarve, just as so many Cape Verdeans, Azoreans, and Algarvians made their homes among the New Bedford and Provincetown fishing communities. There is another family connection here, for Miquinha would surely have crossed paths with Manuel "Manny" Zora in Olhão. Manny ran a Provincetown smuggling crew in the 1920s that my uncle David apparently fell in with. By the time Miquinha came to the Algarve, Manny had returned to his native Olhão, where he roamed the portside bars, the Café Comercial and the Danúbio, telling stories. I have no doubt that Miquinha would have been one of his most appreciative listeners.

Manny was born in Olhão in 1895, but he left on a boat when he was young and settled in Provincetown, on the tip of Cape Cod, around 1910. There he became a somewhat legendary figure, like a character from a Jack London novel. During Prohibition, he became a notorious rumrunner, known to the American Coast Guard as the Sea Fox, for, try as it might, it could never catch him. In the early 1920s, Provincetown had a four-thousand-strong Portuguese community made up of Azoreans and "Bravas" (as Cape Verdeans were known locally, many of them having come from Brava island), as well as Portuguese mainlanders, including 150 or so from Olhão.

The Kennedys rented a summer house nearby, and Manny is said to have taught John, the future president, to sail. It's also said that some of the services Manny provided for John's father, Joseph P. Kennedy Sr., were not entirely aboveboard.

In the 1940s, Manny got involved in politics himself and campaigned up and down the East Coast on behalf of the Progressive Party's candidate for president, Henry Wallace. A little later, he boarded a plane for the first time and went to Washington, D.C., to advocate for a deepwater port project in Provincetown. It's said that after a difficult encounter with Manny, Robert Taft, the Republican senator for Ohio, said he could smell the salt on the seaman's breath.

Manny hung out with many celebrities who spent their vacations in Provincetown. These included the playwright Eugene O'Neill, who based the character of Joe Silva in the trilogy *Mourning Becomes Electra* (1931) on Manny. In the 1937 Hollywood film *Captains Courageous*, Spencer Tracy's character, a Portuguese-ditty-singing fisherman, is likely similarly inspired. Manny was also friends with the actor and singer Burl Ives; Elizabeth Taylor and Eddie Fisher, whom he took sailing for their honeymoon; and Norman Mailer, who liked to discuss the art of fishing with Manny over shots of whiskey dashed with milk. Manny apparently convinced Mailer that he could smell out shoals at high sea. Photographs of the time certainly suggest he had the nose for it, as well as a sun-drenched face, thick hair, and a rugged expression.

There are also photos of him from the 1960s, after he returned to Olhão, hanging out with friends on the rocks at Armona, across the bay, or dining at a restaurant, perhaps recounting tales of Depression-era run-ins with the Mafia. He died in 1979, age eighty-four. The last known image of him sits in an oval frame above his tomb in the Olhão Cemetery, fixing visitors with a sea dog's stare.

I wander around Olhão's old fishing neighborhoods, intrigued by the architecture. The houses are like building blocks, piled one on top of the other and overlapping, with threshing terraces, rooftop patios, and verandas, towers and belvederes. Everything is painted white, with the Portuguese south's traditional blue or yellow borders. I cannot quite identify the street from Pastor's photo, but I feel very much at home in Barreta, as if I've never lived outside its jumbled geometry, its mysterious internal yards, alleyways, and winding back lanes.

I amuse myself with wordplay—*barretar*, "to put on a cap"; *olhar*, "to eye up"—and enjoy getting lost among the streets. Modern cities can be tediously monotonous: straight lines, everything in its place, nothing to muddle or muddy the sense of order. Great effort often seems to have been made to make sure that contact and communication between people are avoided, as if exposure to laughter might be too shocking or overhearing a conversation somehow obscene. Not here; Olhão is a city forged from an ancient sense of humanity.

"Cubes, geometric lines, animal light that trembles and vibrates like the wings of cicada." It might be a description of cubism, but there is no record of Braque or Picasso ever having visited Olhão. This is in fact a line from Raul Brandão's 1923 book *Os Pescadores*

(*The Fishermen*). Brandão describes a community of cunning smugglers, with contraband "passing from rooftop to rooftop—all you had to do was reach out a hand."

Flat rooftops, instead of slanted and tiled ones, gave people broader horizons: outdoor spaces on which to dry fish, corn, and fruit or to breathe in the cool air on a summer's night, but always while gazing out to sea.

Beyond Barreta, Olhão's streets are more perpendicular, but it still feels like being in the medina of a North African town. The narrowness of the streets ensures cool shade on hot summer days. Locals sit on chairs placed at thresholds, as they do in Cape Verde, chatting with neighbors or watching the world go by. I take the opportunity to peek inside their homes, down little corridors that lead from the living room at the front to the bedrooms and the kitchen at the back to, eventually, a backyard.

There is a new five-star hotel on the western edge of town, opened to attract British and German tourists. For years they stayed away because of the stink produced by the eighty-odd fishing canneries. In an industry that employed a sizable chunk of the population, fish were cleaned, beheaded, cooked, and stuffed into tins to be eaten in England, France, or Portugal's African territories, particularly during the Wars of Independence. The industry peaked during World War I, the period from which most of Olhão's more sumptuous buildings date, when cannery owners built homes with lovely art nouveau flourishes. The canneries themselves, meanwhile, were giant sheds with poor ventilation, very little natural light, and no drainage or toilet facilities. These days just one cannery remains, to the east of town beyond the fishing port, tucked in among new industrial units.

The neighborhood of Bairro dos Pescadores, where Miquinha de Djena lived, is a little farther north. It's a poor area, a little chaotic, inhabited by people with dusky skin and hopeless stares.

Youngsters with spiky hair play soccer bare-chested or mess around on bikes. The general sense of poverty is marked. These are the families of poor fishermen working in an industry severely changed and badly hit by recent economic crises. Many of them will survive on government welfare payments. It is no longer the fishing community I imagined. I realize I don't even know the real name of my mother's friend. We called him Miquinha, a common diminutive in Cape Verde that might derive from Marcos, Amilcar, or several other possibilities. Who knows what name he used here, to conduct his Portuguese life?

It's hard to imagine any of these kids having heard of a man who died decades ago, and I leave without asking.

I wander back through Bairro do Levante, with its bourgeois houses painted yellow, pink, and beige and its plant-adorned terraces. These are the buildings built by the cannery managers and wealthy merchants in the early twentieth century. The neighborhood is quiet when I enter, as if all the residents are enjoying a long siesta. The only people I see are tourist couples lingering to admire the lovely facades, details forgotten architects added to bring a touch of nobility to the area and disguise the general poverty of the nation. But as I progress, the streets begin to come alive with the cries of returning schoolchildren and agitated parrots and budgies in cages. Now and then I come across a small plaque commemorating a victory or an honorable mention in the town parade, often several decades ago.

As night falls, I sit down in the park on the waterfront and look across the bay at the inlets in the Ria Formosa and the settlement on Culatra Island. The lights of maritime taxis twinkle as they ride the waves, bringing the last of the day's tourists back to town. In the distance, the Culatra lighthouse sweeps its great flickering light across the water, while children play in the park and an infant takes its first steps, cheered on by its parents. Older boys make the most of the last light to ride bikes around the playground. The rough, commanding voice of a Gypsy family patriarch breaks out from somewhere, ordering that clothes be brought in off the line. Then night rushes in and suddenly everything is strangely calm and silent.

The next morning, I catch the ferry to the island of Culatra. The boat describes a wide arc through the bay, with buoys and safety flags warning of the sandbanks that emerge at low tide. Dozens of shellfish gatherers stand in the shallow water, bent over their buckets, sifting through the mud with hoes. The water's retreat has exposed small stone walls, private plots of some sort for mollusk harvesting. Everywhere rowing boats and motorboats lie stuck in the mud. Farther out, bamboo canes have been wedged into the slush with plastic bowls placed on top, makeshift buoys, presumably, that will come into their own at high tide but now look rather eerie.

I get off the boat and make my slow way through the winding streets of the fishing village. Once on the beach, I walk to the end of the sand where a dozen or so ancient mariners have built shelters well off the radars of European bureaucrats. Taut ropes fasten their sailing boats–cum–floating houses to the shore.

Back on the estuary side, the water has started to rise, filling in grooved channels that run between dunes and bushes. I sit on the ground and listen to the fresh water coming in, invading the dry land inch by inch. I stand up and wait until my feet are completely submerged. In the silence of the island, I hear only my own breathing and the whisper of the water.

I carry on westward toward the lighthouse. I walk along the cement pontoon as if traveling down a road out into the ocean. When I reach the end, the southernmost tip of mainland Portugal, I look out into the Atlantic, toward Africa.

X

He had an instinctive disregard for death and a love of living dangerously. What I perhaps remember most about him are his excesses—the alcohol, the tobacco—along with his very particular notion of goodwill and affection.

My stepfather was a man with a big heart, but at the same time he was incapable of expressing love. I have often asked myself if his marrying my mother was supposed to be some sort of salvation or if it was simply a disaster foretold. He had a sly way of seducing people with his carefree attitude and mad thirst for experience, as if he were riding life like a rodeo. Perhaps he married my mother out of pity and ended up loving her. Even so, he was incapable of answering a direct question from her with anything other than an amazed laugh or an amused grimace. He seemed to see himself as some kind of flawless hero with misunderstood qualities, a view that hardened after half a bottle of brandy.

I think about his constant sense of revolt and rebellion, which seemed to come straight from the heart. He was impulsive, suddenly committed to realizing some absurd idea or fighting to impose his own truth so as to remain loyal to himself. He would stubbornly adopt some strange and ambiguous stance as if his very freedom depended on it, battling to save his shrinking room for maneuver. The next day, all the courage would be gone from him.

We'd watch him drag himself and his slippers to the bathroom to relieve himself of another turbulent night.

He had fixed friends and unreliable affections. He loved good and bad food. He was drawn, irresistibly, to the idea of having a family, but not to the reality of building one. He came into our intimate environment like a ship entering a foreign port on a foggy night, a safe harbor to escape the squalls and storms, not to mention the endless dead hours of staring at the horizon. He seemed capable of anything, but hamstrung by some fear of a terrible threat that hung over him. It was, in a way, fascinating to see his great bundle of energy try to fit into the confined spaces of my mother's home, the way she smothered him with her principles and morals.

These images of him and his presence in the house became blurred during the months he was away at sea, when I became wrapped up again in my childhood routines. Then, toward the end of the year, he would return, and it was always a shock when he ceased to be a concept and became a physical reality again. His presence filled the house not least through the new records he brought back, the sound of salsa, cumbia, and cha-cha-cha blasting joyfully through the house on most mornings. Everything else suddenly became small, overshadowed by his magnitude and magnetism. Looking back, this exuberance might have been a sign of the great effort he was making to live up to people's expectations, our expectations. Forging a family is the most romantic and unpredictable of adventures, but ours had already been formed when he joined it. We'd built it on the few foundations we had, overcoming hardship and despite the absence of a father figure: the quintessential Crioulo story.

My stepfather doubtless had his own poetic notions of what a nuclear family could be, or perhaps he had ambitions of trying to create the childhood refuge he'd never had. But deep down he was not a homely man who burned with conjugal or paternal love, at least not when I lived with him, as a child transitioning to adolescence. His disenchantment was like a bird, starting off up in the clouds, then swooping quickly down to earth. If we made him feel his wings were clipped, he had his job as a lifeline: a few weeks after coming home, he'd be packing his bags again.

He was a cook on a German cargo ship, and if preparing food wasn't exactly a vocation for him, leading a libertarian life plainly was. Perhaps he found freedom in gazing endlessly at the waves and the stars, in following his dreams and being liberated from having to tackle all those difficult Portuguese words. I was never at sea with him to know, but even now I picture him drifting toward the horizon with a smile on his face and a happy heart.

Being a cook, like being a gardener or a librarian, surely ought to make you think about other things than yourself. You don't have to be a poet to gain a little perspective, you just need a dash of ethics. My stepfather was the first person I thought of when I flicked through the *Odyssey* at school. No one else I knew would have been capable of living in the times of antiquity, of overcoming thunderstorms at sea. His Ithaca was our home, which he returned to like a king, even if for only three months of the year. Troy was the sea he did battle with for the other nine months. In my eyes, he was never a mere mortal; there was something epic about him, or at least something unlike civilization as I knew it.

One morning I came downstairs to see him standing at the door talking to a man, a Gypsy I'd never seen before. There was something surreal about the encounter, and, realizing they hadn't noticed my presence, I sat down on the stairs to watch in the half-light. The man took an object wrapped in a cloth out of his trouser pocket and placed it in my stepfather's hands. My stepfather weighed it and unwrapped it. It was a small pistol. He examined it the way an artillery expert might, then wrapped it up again and put it in his front right trouser pocket. From his front left pocket, he took out two or three notes, which disappeared into the other man's hand.

That was the last I saw or heard of the pistol, but the episode instilled in me the idea that men like my father and the Gypsy led lives full of mysterious moments like these. There was a certain romance to their sense of madness and tragedy, a magic to the way they lived their days by night, blowing out the colors as you blow out a candle.

I was too young to think about his strange lifestyle in terms of cause and effect, blame and responsibility. His were the excesses of a man in revolt, snared in his own trap, rebelling not so much against history or the system as against the dictatorship of family life. On the other hand, his attitude introduced me to the duplicity of man: he was at once cynical, proud, and false, generous, sensitive, and quixotic; the whole world was his oyster, yet he was trapped in his own solitude.

In the late 1980s, he showed up at home one day looking decidedly weak, having just been discharged from the hospital on crutches. On a cold and misty day in Hamburg, a car came out of nowhere and knocked him down, dumping him in the snow piled at the side of the road. With almost comic timing, providence had shown that a drunk could not escape the consequences of his reckless actions forever. Newly immobile, he displayed a new kind of passiveness whenever someone talked to him. He would sometimes drag himself, slowly, to sit out in the street or on the veranda, but no longer to pass comment on the rotundity of Portuguese women's backsides. On one occasion, when I was being chased by some bullies, he raised himself from the veranda to brandish his tattooed arms and Danakil Desert warrior haircut, which soon scared the bullies away.

He either wasn't capable of adjusting to or had difficulty in understanding his changed circumstances. He began to inhabit silence like an admission of defeat, for he'd always struggled with or been intimidated by words. But this docility betrayed his sense of self and his notion of what it meant to be a man in the world, his grandiose conception of his own existence. You can't force a man to walk through the wreckage of his life and confront a ruined future. Perhaps he tried, in his silence, to build a truth that he could come to terms with. The cloud he seemed to live under was a sort of unconditional nostalgia.

I remember one day when we went to the beach at Costa da Caparica and, unusually, he came with us. The second he'd finished his lunch, he got up to go and throw himself in the sea, dismissing my mother's warning that he should let his food and drink go down first. The undercurrents at Caparica are strong and the waves were pretty volatile that day, but he came back a few minutes later, dripping wet and laughing his old laugh, lighting a cigarette to seal his sense of satisfaction. It was as if ignoring wisdom and inviting misfortune were some kind of lost and cherished pastime. Or maybe it was just the effect of the sea, which is fairly indulgent of those with self-destructive impulses.

Looking back, I wonder whether he wasn't trying to force the situation with some of his actions, not so much flirting with danger as seeking an escape. He was a man exiled from his hedonistic lifestyle, cut adrift and painfully lost. Despite all this, my mother continued to harbor ambitions that he might be her companion for life. Ignoring his temperamental behavior and base sense of humor, she made countless concessions in order to include him in our lives. She was also the only person with any psychological hold over him. She had a singular means of showing tenderness toward him, which was, itself, a product of freedom.

My relationship with him changed over time, although it was ultimately all in vain. People end up escaping us in the end, slipping through our fingers, and I don't mean this as a moral judgment. Humans are not so different from plants, thriving in the right conditions and surviving in whatever way they can. The resilience of plants can seem astonishing at times, especially to our hyper-lucid, hyperconscious selves, but the way we absorb trauma is perhaps not so very different.

My stepfather always conveyed his power through wrestling bouts. His favorite trick, which neither I nor my brother had an answer to, was to grab you behind the knees and dump you on your back. Then he'd hold out an arm to help you up. These play-fight sessions went on for years, especially when I protested against some unfair rule or other, and were his way of showing us who was boss. Afterward, he'd head off to his room and pick up his two spring grips to train his arm and wrist muscles. He did it with such levity, smiling, admiring his own strength. After half a dozen reps, he'd hand the grips to me.

By the time I was fifteen, I was, at 5'8", taller than him. When he tried to reach my leg with his right hand, he realized I could bring him down. He declared the fight over, a technical draw. Perhaps his status as a stand-in father stirred in him, more than anything else, a sense of duty as my teacher or trainer, able to pass on a little older-man friendship and expertise, but not much more.

I was too young to know about the weight of human failure or futility, the shadow we like to cast over others. Perhaps he was too close for me ever to know him properly. But even a child is able to tell when there's more good than bad in a person.

He would arrive every year with the first chills of December and leave at the end of February. He would always depart at the crack of dawn, coming into the bedroom to kiss us on our foreheads, then vanishing like a ghost. It was a fleeting moment that lingered longer in the memory than it lasted, like the smell of his cigarettes that penetrated every corner of the house. I always pretended I was asleep.

For my twelfth birthday he gave me a calculator. That was the only time I had any sense of the kind of expectations he had for me, if he had any at all. I remember playing soccer and spending the whole game looking to the sidelines to see if he'd come to watch as promised. I soon learned that his promises were to be taken with a pinch of salt.

But I was also no longer the child he'd brought to Lisbon on the *Amélia de Mello*. The world had become more joyful and bright for me; I felt freed from so much fear, anxiety, and stress. It's hard, therefore, for me to portray him without it being a reflection of my own state of mind. In speaking about someone else, we always run the risk of revealing more about ourselves than the subject.

He always had his bobbing kitchen to get back to, pots and pans tied to cupboards to stop them from flying around in choppy waters. Off he went with his happy, seductive smile, the film reel of his real life playing again. My mother would write to him in the afternoon, after putting the *cachupa* pot on to simmer. I always found it hard to picture him replying, which he did do from time to time, sitting in his cabin and composing half a dozen lines of tortuous Portuguese.

5 June 1980, Jersey

Djita, Unforgettable love of my heart

First of all I hope this letter finds you in the perfect health I do so wish for you. I am fine thank God aside from my endless feeling of longing for you. My love I got your letter and I am happy that you are well thanks be to good Jesus Christ. My love I am hearing everything the letter does say but it is not my fault because I send order to send money every months. I have to go to shore to telephone why I have no send money. My love I know you are cross with me for something is not my fault. My love look write my mother to send that papers as quick as possible and leave enough cash for me to get my passport, and also you can write my father for to see if he can send it more quick please. My love every day I have a dream about you but in the end I am far from your feet and I turn in the bed and not find you and I am sad to be a man disappointed to be so far from you and if in Lisbon I have work I not sail in the sea but I must come to the sea and by the end I will be missing you a lot. Sending kisses for my wife and kisses for my children give greetings to your mother and sister and the children of all friends and greetings to anyone who asks of me.

From me husband who loves you to death never forgets you and always remembers his wife always missing her love a lot

Chyau My Love

Many years later, even after their divorce, my mother still allowed him to live in one of the attic rooms of the house. The last time I saw him he was very thin, his cheekbones prominent. His eyesight was failing, his hair receding, and he was almost permanently wrapped in a blanket. He came downstairs only to eat the three meals a day my mother left out for him on the dining room table. When he finished, he went back upstairs and shut himself in his room again. He barely spoke.

When I went in to see him and ask after his health, I got a sort of grunt in response. Several empty bottles of whiskey and brandy lay on the floor and under the bed. There was a nauseating, ingrained smell of sweat mixed with alcohol and tobacco. He reminded me of a homeless guy I used to see under the arches of a building downtown. The reek that came off him seemed to contaminate everything: the curtains, the bedspread, the clothes piled on a chair, even the walls and the slanted ceiling.

There was something else about the smell that I couldn't identify. Something so pungent it cut through the tobacco and the alcohol. It got up my nose and made my nostrils quiver like those of an angry animal. I took a plastic bag and started collecting the empty bottles. When I bent down to reach under the bed, the stench hit me again.

When I stood up, he said, trying to reawaken his old feline cunning, "Look at the state of me. Your mother has me cooped up in here worse than a cannibal!"

I left the room and closed the door behind me, then stood in the corridor mulling over what he'd just said.

It was painful to see him like that. For all his faults, he'd been a man of the world and a rebellious spirit; now he wore the skin of a condemned man, trapped in the tragedy of his existence. He seemed to have been stripped of all imagination, lacking purpose or context, with no love to give or receive.

I thought of all the stories he had to tell, the scrapes and capers he'd gotten into in portside bars around the world, the misadventures of a sailor-cook—stories I would never hear leave his lips. He had never sought to project himself to me through stories, nor to establish some sense of himself through telling them. I would like to have had them for bedtime stories, the sort of tales that must be told and not read, their secrets revealed in the telling. But it was too late now. No matter how much I might have liked to help give him a voice, I sensed our paths had irredeemably separated.

As if on cue, I heard a sudden eruption, a coughing fit that grew and grew and sounded as if it might end in him bursting once and for all. I thought of Nietzsche and wondered if I was condemned to play the role of both son and father for the rest of my life.

I went downstairs and entered the living room, and the moment my eyes met those of my mother, the source of that horrible smell upstairs suddenly came to me: it was urine. The day was definitively spoiled.

TWELVE

"And yet I will show you the most excellent way. If I speak in the tongues of men or of angels, but do not have love, I am only a resounding gong or a clanging cymbal."

The love chapter from 1 Corinthians spills out of the Santa Maria de Lagos Church and drifts over to the old slave market on the other side of the square. The front of the market building is a patio, open to the square on two sides and ceilinged by an upstairs story. The two open sides contain four stone arches, while the walls on the enclosed sides have been covered in a display panel. One is painted yellow, symbolizing gold; the other red, for blood. Four wooden crates hang over the patio on ropes attached to the ceiling, their contents alluding to the cargo of the caravels: malagueta chilies, coconuts and yams, kola nuts, and soil stained yellow to look like gold dust. Photographs of coins from the period, made from copper and silver alloys, adorn the red wall.

The sun is shining brightly on the square, but I have come to Lagos to explore the beginning of a dark chapter in the history of Portugal and humankind. This is the last stage of my trip, a journey determined by a script vaguely mapped out for me by Leopoldina. I can't remember if she's ever been to Lagos, never mind visited its landmarks. But it was here, in this white stone town on the south coast of Portugal, that history, especially the history of the Western world and the Atlantic coasts, became forever tainted.

On August 8, 1444, 235 Africans were brought here on the maiden voyage of the triangular slave trade. They arrived in caravels that displayed the cross of Jesus Christ on their sails. A twenty-first-century replica, the *Boa Esperança*, now sits anchored on the waterfront. A statue of Prince Henry the Navigator, who sponsored the enterprise and was present that day, stands right behind me in the square, which is named after him: Praça do Infante Dom Henrique. I say stands, but in fact he's seated, peering out to sea, and more immediately at a municipal fountain. British and Spanish tourists paddle into the water to have their photographs taken at his feet.

The slave market is now an exhibition space. I join a short queue of people waiting to see a display of historical artifacts unearthed during the building of an underground car park. The interior room beyond the patio is smaller than I'd expected. My attention is immediately drawn to an ivory object in the shape of an animal. It has four legs, but its head is missing, though my guess is it's a goat. Its tail is coiled upward, and from its hindquarters emerges a sort of turret split in two. The item is believed to be an amulet or ornament made in Sierra Leone in the fifteenth century.

Beside it is what is described as the hilt of a metal instrument. Made from bone and iron, it has the form of a headless woman with one hand covering her breasts, the other her stomach. Next come two partially decomposed finger bones, each one sporting the remains of a copper ring, now rusted green. Then there is a delicate frosted-glass flask, also green, perhaps containing the crystallized residue of an ancient elixir. An assortment of jewelry follows: a jet-black beaded necklace, a copper-alloy bracelet, coral earrings. It all dates from the fifteenth century.

For most visitors, the big draw in the room is a Perspex box, little more than one square meter in size, positioned beside the old hearth. Inside the box is the skeleton of a nineteen-year-old man, his upper incisors visible, sharpened according to traditional practices on the West African coast. His legs are shriveled, and his head is turned to one side, as if he were in a deep and eternal sleep. The light from a couple of projectors on the ceiling shows up dozens of child-sized handprints on the Perspex glass.

Behind me, children point out errors in the English translation of *Crónica dos feitos da Guiné* (*Chronicle of the Discovery and Conquest of Guinea*), by Gomes Eanes de Zurara, printed on the wall. Zurara was a chronicler attached to Prince Henry, and he describes August 8, 1444, in some detail.

In the middle of the room, a TV screen manipulates a painting that is supposed to be a portrait of Prince Henry, done on parchment paper, fragmenting his head like a hall of mirrors. Elsewhere, a blown-up diagram depicts the various strata of the earth in order to show the original resting place of the skeleton, where the young man lay hidden in repose for over four centuries.

On my way out, I pass the finger bones with the copper rings again and am struck by how basic the display case is. There's no lock, just a sliding glass door, already open a crack.

The Vale da Gafaria is now a hilltop park with trees that offer shade and a place to relax in lazy contemplation. Few people realize it conceals a centuries-old tragedy. When the Anel Verde underground car park was built here in 2009, 158 skeletons were dug up. Some had been buried with due Christian ceremony, but the vast majority had their hands and arms tied, suggesting they were African slaves, bound up in death as they had been in life.

The area is located just a few blocks from Praça do Infante Dom Henrique, beyond the city walls. This side of town was once known as the Ribeira dos Touros, perhaps because bulls pastured here, but by the fifteenth century it had become the site of a dump and a leper colony—*gafaria* means "leprosarium." A few remains of the leper colony buildings can be seen beside the main entrance to the car park. A footpath winds its way up the hill through the grass and the fledgling olive, palm, fig, and almond trees. A few single women walk their dogs, and tourist couples pose for photographs. There's a plastic bag dispenser for canine waste and a miniature golf course on top of the car park. But there is no information anywhere about the former slave cemetery.

From the top of the little hill, I look out across the blue bay as far as Portimão beach, with its row of modern waterfront hotels. The park's right flank is lined with six-story apartment blocks and a road where cars are parked bumper to bumper. On the park side of the road is a children's playground, a skate park, and what looks to be an open-air auditorium. Alongside the rumble of traffic, I hear crickets and cawing seagulls.

I sit down on the grass and think about the two phalanges with the copper rings, the bodies that they belonged to dumped here, in among the town's trash. Where they among the first 235?

I try to picture that day in 1444. As the half dozen caravels they traveled on approached the promontory, the Africans would first have noticed the two mountains beyond the town, then the hills that led up from the beach. They would have seen the narrow mouth of the Rio Bensafrim that was to welcome them into this terra incognita. The enigmatic sound of church bells would likely have reached them before any sight of the church did, but they would have seen the towers in the ramparts from some distance away. The town would have come gradually into view, built into the foothills on the left bank of the river, the right bank being one vast beach.

Tired and afraid, hungry and thirsty, exhausted from seasickness (most of them never having been in a boat before), they would have watched as their ship entered the river channel. Their arrival would have been greeted with cheers from crowds gathered on the riverbank and from people on barges: friends and family come to welcome home the ships' crew. The sound of joyous reunions would have then faded away slowly as everyone departed and the Africans were left to spend the night on the caravels.

The next morning, they would have been woken, assuming they slept at all, by the chief of the white men shouting instructions. They would have been hurried off the boats and led into a large field, beyond the city limits (today the Rossio da Trindade soccer field and campsite). They would no doubt have assumed they were about to be killed by the bearded, metal-clothed white men, and perhaps even eaten by the people who had started to assemble in a circle around them.

The locals would have had some experience of Moors, but the only knowledge most of them would have had of jet-black people would have come from sailors' yarns told in taverns. Those who went to the field to gawk, some of them traveling from surrounding villages to do so, would have seen the "heathens" with their heads bowed and their faces streaming with tears, exchanging nervous glances or looking to the skies for help. They would have heard them wailing with despair, pain, and sickness.

The chronicler Zurara recorded that some of the Africans struck their own faces with the palms of their hands or pounded the ground with their fists, cursing their misfortune or lamenting their fate in whatever passed for prayer in the customs of their land. The drama of anticipation continued until they began to be divided up, split into five separate groups so that Prince Henry, watching astride his horse on the hillside, could select his share, the royal fifth. The Portuguese officials, led by Lançarote de Freitas, captain of the enterprise, sought to divvy up the weak and the strong evenly, meaning mothers were separated from children, wives from husbands, and so on, family ties an irrelevance. When the Africans realized what was happening, chaos ensued: children clung to their parents, and mothers ran around madly trying to gather up their offspring, only to be dragged away from them, howling and sobbing. The whole sorry spectacle confused the base sentiments of the Christians watching and even aroused the pity of Zurara, for it was a shock to see evidence of such human emotions in those they'd been told were not human.

The prince looked on, implacable, interested only in which set of "pieces" (the terminology used when slaves were logged in ledgers) was to be his, convinced of his superiority and of his divine right to make good Christians of these savage Blacks and Moors.

Those Blacks and Moors would, in a matter of days, be spread out across the Algarve and sent as far away as Seville and Cádiz. The blackest among them were dispatched to Lisbon, as curiosities to titillate the royal court and wow the masses in town squares. All faced the horror of a lifetime spent separated from family, spouses, parents, and siblings, lost forever in an instant.

I try to imagine life as a slave, what it would be to wake up and feel the weight of your life sentence every morning, perhaps feeling disappointed not to have had a providential visit from death during the night. For these people knew there was no way back. There would be the physical pain, a burning desire to cut their chains and break down walls, to stretch out legs and arms, to jump and shout, to run free. And there would be the mental torture: the loss of home, your life becoming an absence, your entire future a void.

The slave asks, silently, *Who do you think you are? What do you know of my rivers, forests, rains, and fresh mornings? Of my children and their smiles? Of my ancestors, my parents and grandparents who hunted and fished in those lands, the same lands their parents and grandparents hunted and fished in. Keep your money, your gold and your silver, your fame and your fortune, your jewelry and your clothes, your hides and your firearms, your horses and your boats, your houses, your tables, your food, your women, your kids, your friends. I watch you carefully every day. On Sundays you put on your hat and go and worship your god, then with your bearded mouth you stand before me and tell me that you own me, that you have my life in your hands. But I am more than my body, exposed and bare as it may be, for I have no need for a thick coat or shoes. I am the eyes of my ancestors that watch you as you walk around with your hands behind your back. Your time will come. There will be no trace left of your terrible hunger and thirst, and your wounds will become a fetid viscous mass. For now, I'm merely trying out words. I live in hope, for I am still breathing. A man lives off his words and deeds, his tongue and teeth, his muscles and strength. Paralyzed by these fetters, I must make do with my words, for even if spoken only to myself, they protect my spirit and prevent me, a man condemned to captivity, from being entirely destroyed.*

I walk back through town, heading for the train station. I pass African men selling sunglasses to white tourist couples, African women braiding the hair of white tourist children. I see the old slave market and cannot resist going back in.

The exhibition room is empty now, and a museum attendant tells me the space will close shortly. I wander around for one last look. When I come to the display case with the objects dug up from the slave cemetery, I stop and look at the phalanges with the copper rings again. I look around me. There's no one else in the room; no one is watching. I slide open the glass and pick up one of the fingers. I hold it in my hand. Then I put it in my pocket.

I head back out into the square and down to the river. I try to visualize the place as a slave port: the gas station, the Intermarché supermarket, Os Mosqueteiros, B&P Real Estate, the wine and beer lounge. A pleasure cruise salesman addresses me in German, trying to sell me a trip to the grottoes, the cliffs, and the beaches.

On the train, I take the little phalange out of my pocket and hold it again. I examine what's left of the ring and imagine a master metallurgist at work in a distant African kingdom. I touch the finger bone, feel its texture and fragility.

The noise of time, the story of a galaxy and a butterfly flapping its wings, comes to me, slowly, in the form of a poem lost in the ether, or a song Leopoldina said she and her classmates used to sing in the schoolyard:

Five Black girls came from far away, all five from Guinea,
They came here from afar, they came here from afar,
Dancing the saricoté, the sarico-té, the sarico-tá.

JOAQUIM ARENA was born in 1964 in São Vicente, Cape Verde. He moved to Lisbon with his family as a young child, going on to study law, before moving back to Cape Verde in 1998, where he worked as a journalist and writer. He now divides his time between Lisbon and São Vicente. He has published three novels, *A Beacon in the Desert*, *The Truth about Chindo Luz*, and *Where the Turtles Fly*. *Under Our Skin* (*Debaixo da Nossa Pele*), which has been widely covered in the Portuguese and Cape Verdean press, is his first full-length work of non-fiction, and his first book to be translated into English.

JETHRO SOUTAR is an English writer and a translator of Spanish and Portuguese. He has translated novels from Argentina, Brazil, Guinea-Bissau, and Portugal, as well as two works by Juan Tomás Ávila Laurel, from Equatorial Guinea. The first, *By Night The Mountain Burns*, published by And Other Stories, was short-listed for the Independent Foreign Fiction Prize. He is a commissioning editor for Dedalus Africa and a cofounder of Ragpicker Press, editing its debut title, *The Football Crónicas*, and its latest, *Refugees Worldwide*. He lives in Lisbon.

Printed in the USA
CPSIA information can be obtained
at www.ICGtesting.com
JSHW082012071123
51628JS00003B/4